1993

Adult Learners on C

We dedicate this book to our friend and colleague
Lila Tabor
on the occasion of her retirement.
Lila epitomizes for us the kind of adult learner described in these pages.
Though she started as an undergraduate in middle age, she completed her
formal education with a Ph.D. in developmental psychology. She joined
our faculty on completing her program and, over the past fifteen years,
she has enlightened us with her insights on how adults mature, and
brightened our lives with her charm and wit.

HBS, MHP, and MLF

Adult Learners on Campus

Henry B. Slotnick
Mary Helen Pelton
Mary Lou Fuller
Lila Tabor

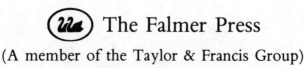 The Falmer Press

(A member of the Taylor & Francis Group)
Washington, D.C. • London

| USA | The Falmer Press, Taylor & Francis Inc., 1900 Frost Road, Suite 101, Bristol, PA 19007 |
| UK | The Falmer Press, 4 John Street, London WC1N 2ET |

First published in 1993

A catalogue record for this book is available from the British Library

Library of Congress Cataloging-in-Publication Data are available on request

  ISBN 0 75070 115 3 cased
  ISBN 0 75070 116 1 paperback

Jacket design by Caroline Archer

Typeset in 10.5/12 pt Bembo by
Graphicraft Typesetters Ltd., Hong Kong.

Printed in Great Britain by Burgess Science Press, Basingstoke on paper which has a specified pH value on final paper manufacture of not less than 7.5 and is therefore 'acid free'.

Contents

List of Tables and Figures

List of Tables and Figures

Foreword

Adult learners have become the new majority on campus. However, yesterday's myths obscure tomorrow's realities, as many people continue to think of higher education students as young people directly out of high school (Millard, 1991). Thus, those of us interested in returning adult students and lifelong learning welcome fresh insights from this book by Slotnick, Pelton, Fuller and Tabor on older than average adult learners at the University of North Dakota.

Returning adults of all ages who compose this new majority include returning students enrolled full time on campus, along with the much larger numbers of adults enrolled part time in degree credit courses that may also be held at evening class or off campus extension locations. When adults who participate in non-credit conferences, institutes, short courses, and other continuing higher education activities are included, the total of these adult learners has for decades outnumbered traditional college students direct from high school. A decade ago, Chickering and Associates (1981) urged that higher education students of all ages be served as adult learners.

Thus, this book by Slotnick, Pelton, Fuller and Tabor is both timely and thought provoking for faculty members who are teaching increasing numbers of older than average students, and for higher education administrators, and even students interested in reflecting on their college experience. Its insights, conclusions, and implications reflect an effective combination of research methods. Included were an empirical survey with an impressive 69 per cent response rate, interviews with younger and older students both at the outset of the study and a three year follow up, and a review of relevant writings that shows how representative the findings are nationwide.

Part of the importance of the North Dakota findings comes from the fact most other research and writing regarding higher education has focused on the parttime student. This study of fulltime undergraduates, graduate, and professional students who are twenty-five years of age and older with its comparison to fulltime traditional age undergraduate, graduate, and professional students helps us appreciate both the ways in which the older than average fulltime students are quite similar to those who are younger and the important ways in which they are different.

One strength of this report is its developmental perspective (based on some of the survey questions, the follow up interviews, and the literature review). This perspective addresses the transactional nature of adult development when personal and situational characteristics interact as past experience affects current activity and future outlook. This was reflected in this study by undergraduate students prior to career commitment who wanted faculty members to confirm them as people, in contrast with more advanced students with a career commitment who wanted faculty members to confirm course content.

This suggests some provocative research hypotheses about similarities and differences between fulltime older than average college students and the more usual adult learners who attend part time. Does the self selection to study fulltime result in returning adults who are similar to younger students? Does the relation between career commitment and study differ for fulltime students in contrast with those who study part time during career transitions later in adulthood? How about the middle aged and older adults, many of whom study for non-occupational reasons? The recent book by Merriam and Caffarella (1991) on *Learning in Adulthood* provides a useful review of such research directions.

A major strength of this report is the emphasis on understanding and being responsive to the diversity of higher education students. Even when there are significant differences related to age, gender, major, educational level, or career stage, there is much overlap. When such characteristics are reflected in differences in experience level or learning style, faculty members should take this diversity into account. The conclusions and recommendations suggest ways in which faculty members can enrich the repertoire of instructional methods and institutional services to better serve the new majority of adult learners.

The useful recommendations address flexibility to help adults cope with competing time and financial demands related to work and family responsibilities. The recommendations also emphasize active learning methods that enable older adults to use their experience for specialized study based on greater seriousness of purpose than many had when they were younger. Using instructional methods for active learning may produce some resistance because active methods may seem more risky to students, and as the findings for law and medical students indicate, people tend to prefer the familiar. Criterion referenced evaluation procedures also help learners assume greater responsibility for their own life-long learning, which is easier for people of any age who have some background on the topic. These conclusions regarding responsiveness to student diversity and development apply to learners of all ages. These are useful insights for higher education students, teachers, and administrators.

Alan B. Knox
University of Wisconsin

References

CHICKERING, A.W. and ASSOCIATES (1981) *The Modern American College*, San Francisco: Jossey-Bass.
MERRIAM, S.B. and CAFFARELLA, R.S. (1991) *Learning in Adulthood*, San Francisco: Jossey-Bass.
MILLARD, R.M. (1991) *Today's Myths and Tomorrow's Realities*, San Francisco: Jossey-Bass.

Preface

The Adult Learner Consulting Group

We represent the Adult Learner Consulting Group — a dozen or so faculty and graduate students at the University of North Dakota who share a general interest in the related processes of learning and teaching, and a specific concern about the ways older-than-average students learn and the instructional methods most appropriate for them. Our interests in education generally come from training (many of us have degrees in psychology and education), experience (both teaching and researching educational issues), and our view that, as professionals, we constantly strive to improve ourselves and our profession — in this case, college teaching.

But it was our specific interest in the older learner that initially brought us together. Because of our experiences as both older learners and teachers of older learners, we were aware of a certain class of problems on campus: 'The professor doesn't understand that I have responsibilities beyond being a student' and 'I don't see how what we're learning relates to my professional needs' were examples of older students' complaints, while 'Older students tend to take over the class' and 'Older students seem to question pretty much everything that comes up in class' were concerns frequently voiced by faculty. The Adult Learner Consulting Group wished to do what we could to help resolve them.

Our activities were usually co-sponsored by the Office of Instructional Development on campus and always enjoyed the support of the Vice President for Academic Affairs. These offerings ranged from group activities such as faculty seminars on older students to invitations to individual professors who might bring their concerns to our meetings so we could discuss them and offer our best suggestions for their resolution. The activities were all well received by a certain number of colleagues although, over time, we addressed their needs and found ourselves playing to smaller and smaller audiences. What we now needed, we decided, was a shift in emphasis, a shift that would allow us to continue addressing our general interests in education and our specific concerns about older students. We wanted to shift from a reactive, problem-solving approach to a proactive, research-based approach allowing us to address a different set of colleagues, colleagues who would profit from an increased knowledge of older students and who recognized the value of empirically-based research. These are people studying the field of adult learning generally, scholars and practitioners in adult education in particular.

We also wondered whether some kind of written materials might be of use to them, written materials comparing and contrasting older and traditional-aged students and describing those educational approaches holding the greatest promise of good instructional outcomes.

We also expected these materials would be of use to students taking courses in higher education, graduate students contemplating college teaching positions, and new faculty assuming their first teaching responsibilities.

Goals of This Study

How, then, do we describe older students? Our first inclination was to go to the literature — a literature we already knew well from preparation for our seminars — and produce a composite picture of older students. We'd talk about their needs (e.g., why they elect to enroll in the first place), their psychosocial developmental status (e.g., unlike more traditional students, they'd already separated themselves from their families of origin), and the instructional formats that worked best with them (e.g., older students liked discussion methods, the literature indicated).

It wasn't clear, though, whether our students were like those the literature proposed to describe. First, many studies were methodologically flawed (they were based on self-selected samples of students, for example), and second, because of the remoteness of North Dakota, we were concerned that our population of students might be different from those found on other campuses. Certainly we could (and did) critically review the literature, but we were still left with the question of whether those findings described our students. We decided the appropriate solution to our problem was empirical in nature, and we embarked on the study described here.

We set out to address three specific goals: (i) to describe older-than-average students enrolled full-time, (ii) to compare older-than-average students with traditional-age students on campus, and (iii) to compare older-than-average students with their counterparts nationally. And so we proceeded.

However, once the study was begun, we realized the data we were collecting addressed broader issues. First, we'd noted that much of the Adult Learner literature was based on supposition about both traditional-age students and older learners. More specifically, the hypotheses presented, while not necessarily incorrect, were often based on such things as personal experiences or generalizations from theory which hadn't benefitted from rigorous empirical investigation. A good example here is the notion that older learners — in contrast to traditional-age students — prefer discussion methods because it gives them an opportunity to share their experiences and learn from the experiences of others. How do we know that? Is it possible the finding emerged from asking particularly verbal older students why they liked discussion?

We hoped to avoid these kinds of threats to internal validity, and we felt we could by mounting a study addressing its goals in as scientifically rigorous a manner as possible within the constraints of limited time and money. The technical description of our research methods is provided in Appendix A, and a briefer description appears in Chapter 3.

Second, we elected to look at both older learners and those of more traditional ages. We did this to enrich our descriptions; not only could we describe older learners, we could also sketch a portrait of younger ones and so highlight important similarities and differences between these two groups.

And third, we moved to protect the study's external validity. Specifically, and as noted earlier, many studies in the literature used self-selected samples or samples of people available to the researcher, samples which may or may not have been representative of the population of adult learners. We avoided this difficulty by using a random procedure for identifying subjects from our adult population; in this way, our conclusions would escape such threats to our study's validity. In addition, we present information in Chapter 3 showing how the population of adult learners at the University of North Dakota is representative of adult learners in the United States.

The result of addressing these three issues was that we now viewed the goals of the study as:

Characterizing the student body generally Because we collected data on all students — regardless of age — we could both (a) compare and contrast different groups of students, and (b) generalize our findings to the population of all students.

Providing an integrated picture of students While most studies in the literature looked in detail at particular aspects of students, this study strove to be more catholic in its coverage. This meant our findings considered students — regardless of age — as multidimensional individuals whose roles as employees or spouses, say, impinge on their activities as students.

Contrasting with students nationally The last goal concerned whether our University's students were like those on other campuses. While we already knew this was not the case in some ways (e.g., non-coeducational institutions, colleges, and schools serving more culturally diverse populations than ours), we did not know the answer in terms of the spectrum of issues describing students in higher education — one example being why people elect to go to school. If our students are no different from those at other schools in the reasons they attend college, then our findings have greater generalizability than would be otherwise the case. We've examined the population of adults at the University of North Dakota in Chapter 3, with particular reference to ways in which it is similar to other higher education institutions in the United States.

It is against the background of these three goals that our study is best understood.

Organization of This Book

We've divided this book into two sections. The first reviews the literature on adults with particular reference to adults as learners (Chapter 1) and developmental changes adults realize with particular focus on those changes likely to occur while they attended the university (Chapter 2). With this background information presented, the book moves to the second section dealing with the results of our study.

Chapter 3 presents a brief description of the survey methodology we used (as noted, there is a lengthier technical description in Appendix A) and describes the considerable evidence that our university is typical of higher education institutions in the USA. The chapter also introduces thirteen students we interviewed after the survey was completed, students coming from the strata from the population we sampled. These people were of importance to us because they provided one source of the interpretations presented in this book; we provided them with survey results and asked them what, given their ages and educational backgrounds, they thought our findings meant. (Since we quote these students regularly, we also offer a brief introduction to them immediately following this Preface. Some readers will find these thumbnail sketches a useful reference when they encounter these students throughout the sequel.)

We'd like to add a bit more about these students. Even though we make no claim that they are a representative sample of students at our university, we found them reflective and their observations insightful. The result is that their contributions added an important dimension to this study, a dimension tying our results firmly to the human experience of attending the university.

The information in Chapter 3 on methods, the University of North Dakota, and the thirteen students is preparation sufficient to the task of reading and understanding the study's findings which appear in Chapters 4 and 5. Chapter 4, entitled 'Issues related to college attendance', describes topics bearing on teaching and learning but which are not parts of it. These topics include why people attend college and the kinds of demands made on them while they are in attendance. The chapter ends with implications of interest to those who teach university students.

Chapter 5, entitled 'Issues related to teaching and learning', parallels the last chapter but deals specifically with concerns about how people learn at the university. The topics considered here range from those observable in the classroom (such as preferred instructional styles and attributes of best and worst teachers) through those that are important but more peripheral to the classroom (support services and personal strengths and weaknesses are examples). This chapter also ends with implications for those who teach.

Chapter 6 takes all the implications we've identified and organizes them into a series of thirteen recommendations. These recommendations, though grounded in the results of our study, are not necessarily novel; a number of them have been proposed by other writers and those authors are cited with appreciation.

In addition to the recommendations, we also offer suggestions on how to implement them in the classroom. We offer the suggestions primarily for readers who are new to teaching adults, though we hope more experienced readers will find at least some of them new and interesting. We offer them because an important characteristic of adult learners (such as the people we expect will be reading these pages) is practicality. In addition to presenting an integrated picture of adult learners on campus, this book also provides some teaching techniques that can be used in class tomorrow.

Chapter 7 is both a summary and an epilogue. It is an epilogue in describing where our thirteen interviewed students are now and a summary in that we discuss our study's findings as they appeared in these students' lives over the three years since they were initially interviewed.

Finally, we provide two appendices we hope will be helpful to readers with specific interests. As noted, our methodology is presented in Appendix A (along with a copy of our survey instrument and the letters sent to respondents) while Appendix B contains an annotated bibliography of books on adults and adult learning.

Appreciations

Though we are the people most directly responsible for the study reported here, the study could not have been done without the efforts of many others. Funding for the study was provided by the University of North Dakota's Faculty Research Committee, and we would like to specifically acknowledge Richard Landry who chaired the committee at the time. Dick, as Director of the Bureau of Educational Research and Services, also graciously provided in-kind support for the survey.

Much support in the form of money, supplies, and clerical staff assistance came from three offices on campus. The first is the Division of Continuing Education headed by Dean Robert Boyd. Without Bob's help, the project would have been impossible. The second is the Office of Medical Education and Research Services where Dorothy Elston, the departmental secretary, provided an important part of the clerical support for the project. And third, Karla Glick of the Division of Biomedical Communications did her usual excellent job of preparing the figures included in these pages.

Our colleague and friend, Robert King, read our manuscript at different times in its evolution, and we are appreciative to him for suggestions which were invariably helpful and frequently witty. This book is better for Bob's efforts.

We also offer a special thank you to Doreen Keable who, as a graduate student, contributed much time and effort to this project.

Finally, we would like to acknowledge Falmer Press's Managing Director, Malcolm Clarkson, for his counsel. We'd like to note that in his experience seeing books through from inception to publication, he'd never seen a book written by a committee (or at least one where the committee members still spoke to one another when the writing was completed). On the basis of his experience and ours, we commend this book to readers as one which was written by a committee, a committee whose members still enjoy each others' company.

Indeed, we've enjoyed working on this project since its beginning, and we hope the pleasure we've had in completing it comes through in our prose.

Thirteen People who Helped Us Understand Adult Learners

In addition to the mailed survey providing the bulk of the findings we report in this book, we interviewed six *Young Adults* (age twenty-four and younger) and seven *Adults* (age twenty-five and older) enrolled as full-time students in three different colleges (*Undergraduate*, *Graduate*, and *Professional* — law and medicine). Though we interviewed all thirteen people using the same protocol, we do not report each person's answer to each question. Rather, we reviewed the answers to see what insights they provided into the survey's findings, and we offer quotes and other observations from the interviews as appropriate.

We are indebted to the Adult students for sharing their experiences and perspectives with us, and to the Young Adults whose views helped us clarify what we learned about the Adults. We hope that readers of this book will come to know these students as people and appreciate them as much as we do.

Adult Learners

Jerry is 31 years old and in his last year of law school. Prior to attending law school, *Jerry* worked as a laborer in the western North Dakota oil fields and decided to return to school when oil prices declined.

Robert, a 35-year-old medical student, is like Jerry in returning to school with much experience behind him. Robert is an ordained minister who is also married and has two young daughters.

Amber is a 40-year-old law student who is married but has no children. Prior to attending law school, she had 14 years as a nurse in a variety of settings.

Unlike the preceding students whose studies are in the professions, *Steve* is a graduate student in the College of Business and Public Administration. He is 34 years old, married and has children.

Marlys, a 25-year-old psychology graduate student from a small town, is married and has a baby. She currently works about twenty hours a week as a GTA and spends about forty hours a week at cooking, cleaning, and other domestic responsibilities.

The last two people are undergraduates. *Jimmy* is a high energy 40-year-old who retired recently from the military. He thus exemplifies an important reason for returning to school — a change in occupation (Apps, 1981).

Finally, *Naomi* is a 47-year-old undergraduate who has lived in a variety of places and held a number of interesting jobs. She and her husband (also a student) have one child who is a college freshman at another institution.

Young Adult Learners

Martin is a 23-year-old law student who majored in accounting as an undergraduate and chose to go directly to law school. In addition to being a student, he clerks for a law firm, working approximately twenty to twenty-five hours per week.

Britt is a 23-year-old medical student who went directly from high school to college and then to medical school. Though she has never worked fulltime, she has held a series of part-time jobs and is now a member of the National Guard — a commitment requiring her to spend one weekend a month and two weeks during the summer in military training.

Rhonda is a 22-year-old graduate student in the University's Center for Teaching and Learning (our college of education) who works eight hours a week as a graduate teaching assistant.

Daniel, aged 23, is a single graduate student who works about twenty-five hours a week at an outside job.

Charles, a 19-year-old unmarried undergraduate majoring in engineering, is also a National Merit Scholar and an Eagle Scout.

Billie Jo is a 22-year-old unmarried undergraduate in engineering who is looking forward to graduating soon. She is somewhat of an entrepreneur: As an undergraduate, she bought a small house and has rented out a room to help cover expenses, has worked as a freelance house painter, managed a bingo hall, and worked with the Special Olympics.

These thirteen people will be quoted again in the sequel. When they are mentioned, their names will be followed by a pair of letters indicating their Age and College. Charles, for example, will be cited as *Charles (YA,U)* meaning he is a Young Adult and an undergraduate, while *Steve (A,G)* means Steve is an Adult enrolled as a Graduate student. The letter *P* will identify those students in the Professional schools of law and medicine.

Part I

A Background on Adult Learners

Introduction

Part I of this book provides background on Adult Learners from the perspectives of both how they learn and changes in cognitive ability and identity. Chapter 1 ('Adult learners') describes attributes of adults with particular reference to aspects of them and their lives which impact on what and how much they learn. Of particular interest is *Andragogy*, a framework for viewing adults and adult learners in contrast to pedagogy — the ways in which children learn. Some attributes important in this contrast include the reasons for learning, the ways in which students participate in their learning, the goals learners have, and the roles played by teachers.

Chapter 2 ('Adult development') attends particularly to questions of cognitive and identity development. These topics are important because they are intimately related to the changes that occur in students — whether Young Adult or Adult — due to the experience of attending the university. The issues of cognitive and identity changes will figure prominently in the conclusions we draw from our study and the recommendations we make at the book's end.

Chapter 1

Adult Learners

Confessions of a 31-year-old Law student:

> I was a typical teenager — I didn't know what I wanted to do. As an undergraduate I pursued two or three different courses of study. I think that is pretty normal, unless you're really certain what you want to do, and I wasn't. I think that in general terms, the older you get, the more you realize that you could have been a lot more efficient — done a better job. But you just can't explain that to somebody; they have to experience it themselves. As you mature, you realize that if you really want something, you're responsible and you're going to have to work for it. Once you've been out in the world, you realize that it is going to take a lot of work to reach your goals.
>
> I feel much more in control of my life than I did when I was a traditional age student, although I think Adult learners feel much more self-imposed pressure than younger students. The person who is first in our law school class is thirty-two, I am second, the person who is third is younger (twenty-six) but took a couple of years off, and the individual that is fourth is a civil engineer [who] has been out at least half a dozen years. I think that this is fairly indicative of the type of pressure that we [Adult learners] put on ourselves.
>
> *Jerry*

Introduction

This quote suggests a number of things about the Adult learner: they know what they want, they're willing to work hard to get it, and there are a number of them around. Though we will return to issues such as Adult learners' needs and the way these students approach learning later

3

in this chapter, we will first look at the size of the Adult learner population and the rate at which that population is growing.

The size of the Adult population is considerable (at the beginning of the academic year in which we conducted our study, 1.6 million of the 7.2 million fulltime students were over 24 years of age. This means that, on average, 22 per cent of the students in our classes are Adult learners. What is more, the number of the Adult students in college is increasing at an impressive rate, and demographers project that, as we move toward the year 2000, the largest increases in the college student population will continue to be the 25–44 year old group.

> The number of older students has been growing more rapidly than the number of younger students. Between 1970 and 1985, the enrollment of students under age 25 increased by 15 per cent. During the same period, enrollment of persons 25 and over rose by 114 per cent. In the latter part of this period from 1980 to 1985, enrollments of students under 24 decreased by 5 per cent, while the enrollment of persons 25 and over increased by 12 per cent. (Snyder, 1991, p. 47)

Even in the face of dramatic increases in the adult student population, professors often fail to address sufficient attention to older students. We suspect that some of these faculty see the numbers of older students as having no educational implications while others consider this growing population a short-lived phenomenon. Both of these views are wrong: Older students are a growing, important, vital, and permanent feature of the university.

Adult learners bring a variety of life experiences with them to the university, experiences giving them a perspective and a sense of purpose not found in the younger student's tool kit for dealing with and profiting from higher education. These students know who they are, they know what they want, and they have a pretty good idea of how the system works. They are, in a phrase, sophisticated consumers who will make their needs known and will work hard at having them met. This means that as the numbers of adult learners increase, faculty will have to become more sensitive to their personal, academic, and professional needs. And skillful teachers will also find ways to draw on these students' experiences in the process of responding to their needs.

Who Are Adult Learners?

Who are these adult learners? What is known about them? And how do we organize our thinking about them? The term 'Adult learners' ('older-than-average' is often used as a synonym) refers to persons 25 years old and older who are engaged in learning experiences. Those experiences may be as informal as casual pursuit of a subject of interest or joining others to learn new skills, or they may be as formal as taking a night class or pursuing a degree program. Our particular interest in adult learners addresses the formal end of the continuum — adult college students, whether undergraduate or more advanced.

While there are excellent studies pertaining to the adult students (e.g., Cross, 1981; Apps, 1981), contemporary beliefs about the education of adults nevertheless include a lot of speculation. These beliefs might be labeled the 'folk wisdom' of adult education because they are agreed upon and accepted even though they are untested. In studying students on our campus, we wished to limit ourselves to those assertions which were empirically defensible, and we did this by addressing the three goals of this study: identifying certain characteristics of traditional age and adult students generally; using these characteristics to provide an integrated picture of students on campus; and contrasting our population of students with students nationally.

Terminology

Given these goals, we decided to stratify the population of students on campus, a task we approached by considering two attributes of students: their ages and college in which they are enrolled. Considering age, and as noted earlier, we called the older-than-average students (25 and over) *Adults* and the traditional-age students (24 and younger) *Young Adults*. Since our study included Graduate and Professional students (that is, law and medical students) who are commonly over 24 years of age, this terminology is highly appropriate; it allowed us to avoid an artificial distinction (traditional *versus* older-than-average) for these groups.

As we mentioned earlier, we also stratified the population of students by College (Undergraduate, Graduate, and Professional) producing six strata when Age (Young Adult and Adult) is considered as well. We anticipated that dividing the population in these ways would provide informative contrasts yielding useful insights into the similarities and differences among student groups.

Perspective on Adults and Adult Learning

Our view of the adult learner was influenced by our adopting a humanistic perspective toward teaching and learning: We believe there is a natural tendency for people to learn and that learning will flourish if a nourishing, encouraging environment is provided. We also believe that, although there is great diversity in the nature and lives of adults, there are predictable patterns (developmental stages, for example) experienced by most adults. This view is hardly new to those familiar with the human development literature, a literature enriched by Carl Jung, Robert Havighurst, Erik Erikson, Jean Piaget, and Daniel J. Levinson, among others.

We were also influenced by research on adult learners, particularly the later work of Malcolm Knowles (e.g., 1980, 1984). Knowles, based upon his research and his reading of the literature, feels that there is sufficient information available 'to warrant attempts to organize it [the available information] into a systematic framework of assumptions, principles, and strategies' (1984, p. 7). His construction of such a framework, called *andragogy*, is concerned with teaching adults (*versus* pedagogy which is concerned with teaching children), and combines elements of humanistic psychology with a systems approach to learning. John Dewey, E.H. Erikson, Jerome Bruner, Abraham Maslow, and Carl Rogers give andragogy its theoretical and philosophical bases.

Some theorists correctly question whether andragogy is a theory (Cross, 1981; Brookfield, 1986; Haertree, 1984; Houle, 1972), and Knowles (1984) responded by saying, 'I don't know if it is a theory . . . I feel more comfortable thinking of it [andragogy] as a system of concepts . . .' (pp. 7–8). And, indeed, andragogy works well as a system of concepts providing a perspective on the adult learner.

Andragogy Versus Pedagogy

Concept of the Learner

As Knowles (1980) views pedagogy, the learner is a dependent person and the teacher has full responsibility for making all curricular decisions. The learner in andragogy, in contrast, is self directed; these learners typically make their own decisions concerning their educations — as demonstrated by *Jerry (A,P)* in the quote at the beginning of this chapter. This was particularly true for our Adult population with Young Adults approaching this position.

In pedagogy, learners are passive and curricular material is generally transmitted to them by lecture, assigned readings, and audio-visual presentations. Further, learners have had few life experiences to use in interpreting what they are learning. In contrast, andragogy attributes to the adult learners many and varied life experiences (due both to having lived longer and having played a variety of roles such as student, parent, employee, and so on) which they bring into the classroom along with specific needs to be addressed by instruction. The result is that Adult learners are more active in pursuing their learning and better able to see the importance and limitations of what they learn. We find that Young Adults appear to be in a transition between the children described by pedagogy and the Adults described by andragogy.

In situations appropriate to pedagogy, the learner is presented with a curriculum for a given grade level which implies that readiness for learning is largely a function of grade (age). The fact that what a child needs to learn is determined by grade level is simply another way of saying that a child of one age studies this, one of another age studies that. Curricular decisions, in other words, are made for the students. The andragogical model, in contrast, assumes that adults become ready to learn when they feel a need to know or have a need to perform more effectively in some area of life. In other words, adults make decisions about when children are ready to learn, and adults also make decisions about when they are ready to begin their own learning.

There are important ways in which the undergraduate (and even the law and medical) curricula are like the pedagogical curricula just described. At first appearance, students simply present themselves and are exposed to whatever the curriculum has to offer. This is much less the case for older students who have generally more well-developed reasons for wanting to take specific courses or enroll in entire curricula.

Children and adults also have different orientations to learning. For the child, stress is placed on learning outcomes rather than the process of learning — as is the case with the instruction of Adults. In short, the orientation in pedagogy is subject-centered and the goal is mastery of the content. But because adults enter the learning environment with a specific need to know, their orientation is more life (process) centered than product (content) centered. Thus the Adult, having learned, is in a better position to continue learning than is the child.

We will show, in a subsequent chapter, that Young Adults are typically in the process of separating from their families of origin and thus are in the process of gaining Adults' life experiences. Because this process has just started for them, they do not yet have the rich backgrounds enjoyed by the Adults with whom they share their classes. (This last point can be seen at the end of this chapter in the biographies of the Young Adults we interviewed for this study. Some Young Adults, like *Charles*, are just beginning this process while others, like *Rhonda* and *David*, are further along.)

There is an important difference in the motivation of Adults and children toward learning. Children are motivated by external pressures (parents, teachers, grades, and so on) while Adults are more internally motivated. Knowles states that, 'Although it is acknowledged that adults will respond to some external motivators — a better job, a salary increase, and the like — the andragogical model predicates that the more potent motivators are internal — self-esteem, recognition, better quality of life, greater self-confidence, self-actualization, and the like' (1984, p. 12). Adults learn because they want to — not because someone else wants them to. As noted, we believe that Young Adults are in a transitional state approaching the motivational status of Adults.

Implications

Knowles describes Adult learners as self-directed people who are responsible for their own lives and who need to be recognized as such. We agree with this view and feel that it carries educational implications for faculty who teach Adults. First, Adults have had a multitude of varied life experiences making them, as a group, highly diverse. And this, combined with the facts that Adults are internally motivated and appear in learning settings with their own goals for attending, means they have a greater need for individualization of the instruction they receive.

Given that Adults recognize their own needs and see themselves as responsible for seeing that those needs are addressed, it is not surprising that Adults seek learning when they are ready. They also expect their needs to be addressed by that learning, and this means faculty must take these needs into consideration when organizing curricula and instruction for Adults.

Second, Adults normally reserve to themselves the option of deciding to participate in learning experiences, decisions they make based on whether they feel participation will address their needs. This, in turn, implies that Adult learners must understand both what the outcomes of instruction will be and how those outcomes will address their reasons for seeking instruction.

Finally, Adult learners rely more heavily than Young Adults on internal rewards for their efforts. They will decide whether they've been successful or not. In a word, 'knowing one's own needs, deciding when and how to address them, and responding to internal rewards are characteristics of adult learners worthy of educators' attention' (Cross, 1981, p. 227).

Andragogy and This Study

The visibility of andragogy has heightened awareness of the need for answers to three major questions: Is it useful to distinguish the learning needs of adults from those of children?, What are we really seeking: Theories of learning? Theories of teaching? Both? Does andragogy lead to researchable questions that will advance our knowledge in adult education? (Cross, 1981).

Of Cross's questions, only the first was of particular interest to us. Not only did we ask if it was useful to distinguish the learning needs of Adults from Young Adults, but we first needed to determine if there actually were differences. Does andragogy posit a clear cut dichotomy between the adult and child learner?

Being neither a defensive nor a stubborn sort, Knowles readily admits that he's fine tuned his andragogical assumptions over the years. What he once envisioned as unique characteristics of adult learners, he now sees as innate tendencies of all human beings, tendencies that emerge as people mature. (Feuer and Geber, 1986, p. 35)

If there are no clear-cut distinctions between Adult and younger learners, and if there are detectable differences, then it's appropriate to ask what they are and how they apply to teaching — particularly teaching Adults. Indeed, if we had to sum up the goal of this study in a single sentence, it would be the answer to the question, 'Where are the boundaries between teaching and learning appropriate for Adults *versus* teaching and learning that describes younger people?'

An Introduction to the Adult Learner

In contrast to the research evidence, there is a lingering myth that all adults' abilities to learn are somehow impaired by the passage of time (McCluskey, 1976). In fact, adults returning to college are quite capable students though they do exhibit a set of characteristics that can be mis-interpreted as evidence of inability). They generally do not like competitive class activities, for example; they do not normally feel the need to develop warm, personal relationships with the faculty or their peers; and they have a lessened concern for speed in learning since they are more concerned about accuracy (Knox, 1977).

Adult learners do, however, feel the classroom is a comfortable setting for testing new ideas and challenging viewpoints presented by teachers and students (Schmidt, 1984). They also prefer a curriculum that is learner-centered with learning episodes capitalizing on the students' experiences. Finally, they are also self-directed in motivation, and problem-centered in their orientation to learning (Conti, 1984).

> Because adults typically want to use what they learn soon after they learn it, it is usually easy to establish the connection between specific learning activities and the area of performance to which the new knowledge is to be applied. (Knox, 1977, p. 408)

The information in the preceding paragraph is nicely summarized by Knox who points out that Adults actively seeking to enhance their proficiencies tend to think of themselves as 'users of, instead of recipients of, education' (1980, p. 79).

A number of writers in the field feel there is no one best instructional technique to use in teaching adults (Draves, 1980; Dubin and Okin, 1982; Mackie, 1981; Even, 1982; Moore, 1982). They feel that individual differences, and not age, dictate preferred instructional styles for Adults (also see Beder and Darkenwald, 1982). However, while classroom practices may not differ, the way students participate in them likely does vary with age. Specifically, Apps (1981) feels that differences among students (such as those noted earlier) mean that the same activities will receive different kinds of participation from Young Adults and Adults.

As noted earlier, Adults learn best when they feel a need to learn and when they have a sense of responsibility for what, why, and how they learn (Brookfield, 1986). It is possible, though, that andragogical techniques (e.g., experiential learning) are superior to pedagogy for children as well as adults, simply because they support good teaching practices without regard to whether they address the needs of a particular age group. Evidence for this view is provided by research showing that children learn best under these conditions (Hamachek, 1986).

Since our interest is the Adult learner, we are most interested in descriptors of this population. If Knowles' (1984) descriptions of good teaching also apply to other groups of learners, so much the better.

Chapter 2

Adult Development

The Differences Between Young Adult and Adult Students

I think . . . really . . . it deals with your need to be a part of a group or work directly with the other students and that type of thing. At least from what I've seen with older than average students . . . they come to their classes and they go. They may go to the library and study or they may go home and do their work at home. They don't have this need to sit and BS with the students or go to the hockey game or go out and do this and that. You know, they've got their family, they've got a whole life outside of school and that that they've been working on for however many years. They just don't need [the socializing], I guess. *Daniel (Y,G)*

Daniel's contrast of Adult students' independence and Young Adult students' social needs has been made before; it is part of what is already known about changes occurring in people as they mature. And it is true that what is already known can be a good guide to what is to be learned. Developmental issues, the topic of this chapter, play the role of the already known material, and we present them here as a guide to understanding what we have learned in our study — the material in the chapters to follow. We will use developmental issues as a way of both identifying similarities among and differences between our Young Adults and Adults, and as a way of understanding the patterns in the answers to questions we report later.

It is a mistake to think of adult development as simply the progression of a person from one stage to the next. There is a progression, of course, but it occurs for each individual against the background of the environment within which that individual lives. Interestingly, recognizing the progression — and then appreciating its importance in the lives of adults — is a recent phenomenon. As Knox (1977) observes:

In earlier eras, attention to human growth and development was focused on childhood and adolescence, and adulthood was considered a period of stability. Rapid social change, pluralistic and egalitarian values, and an aging population have shifted our attention to the dynamics of the process by which adult life unfolds.

In fact, adulthood is composed of ample portions of outward adaptation and internal change, along with the established patterns of interest and activity that appear to be so stable over the years. We gain useful insights into adult functioning by considering the mix of stability and change that occurs during adulthood. Some changes, such as increased competence or decreased speed, occur gradually. Others, such as marriage or retirement, occur more abruptly. As a result of changes in physical condition, personality, and environmental conditions, adult performance is continually modified as the individual interacts with his or her social and physical environment. (p. 1)

Knox is correct, of course; adult development occurs in a variety of ways simultaneously. However, the developmental issues we consider most appropriate to our study address cognition and identity. *Cognitive development* describes differences among people of different ages in terms of the ways in which they 'think', and, as such, tells about the ways in which they view and interact with the world in which they live. More specifically, cognitive development describes changes over time in the ways people perceive the problems they face, organize their thinking, and produce solutions to those problems.

In a collegiate environment, for example, the demands of upper division undergraduate courses require that students deal with highly abstract notions and consider the fact that perceptions of reality vary from expert to expert. Successful college students are capable of doing both of these: They can deal with abstractions and they can accept the fact that each expert's view of reality has merit and must, therefore, be considered. This is relativistic thinking, a kind of thinking which allows them to interact successfully with the otherwise confusing intellectual environment in which they learn.

Identity development is the second issue in this chapter. *Marcia* describes *identity* as a 'self-structure — an internal self-constructed, dynamic organization of drives, abilities, beliefs and individual history' (Damon, 1983, p. 325). Like the development of cognition, identity development speaks to how people interact with their environments. Its voice, however, is the voice of the person — who the individual really is who sits in the upper division course and how that person relates to both the course and the rest of the world.

Both cognition and affect are involved in the search for identity. People use cognitive strategies to determine what roles they will play in life and how they can attain such goals. And during this process, they are concerned about how they will 'fit in', how others view them, and how competent they will be. In other words, identity is also important because it has an impact on the ways people feel about themselves and thus how they will approach and interact with the world in which they live.

Timing of Development

Adult identity development begins in earnest in late adolescence — about the lower boundary of our Young Adults age group — and does not necessarily end with the beginning of adulthood (Damon, 1983). Indeed, it often continues into the thirties and middle age. This is particularly true of the career aspect of identity since many of us do not settle on and then settle into a profession until our children are almost grown.

Though not perfectly congruent, cognitive and identity development proceed hand in hand. As noted, both are developmental in nature (i.e., both admit of stages with the successful resolution of early stages' tasks being necessary for successfully approaching later stages), and both bear on how individuals cope with their worlds. And — quite importantly — both are influenced by many of the same issues including how the world deals with the individual and the kinds of commitments each individual makes in the process of growing. Not surprisingly, this commitment, with its concomitant set of values and other moral considerations, is a very important issue, which we will consider in greater detail later in this chapter.

In the pages that follow, we will describe aspects of cognitive and identity development in Young Adults and Adults, drawing on the experiences of the thirteen people we interviewed; we will use excerpts from those interviews to illustrate important points. The conclusions we reach, then, will draw on our interviewees' lives, but, in fact, they will generalize to the population of interest to us: Adult learners.

Cognitive Development

Piaget's Theory

Jean Piaget's theory of cognitive development is both well accepted and bears directly on the developmental issues described here. The highest level of functioning he described, formal operations, is often but not always reached by students attending college. Students who are formally operational have the ability to consider both what is real and what is possible, they can examine relationships among things by thinking about them, and they can use both logic and experimentation to determine which of the relationships they had thought of are, in fact, correct (Flavell, 1963). In other words, not only can they use symbols to represent things in their minds, they can apply propositional thinking to manipulate those symbols in the process of hypothetico-deductive ('if . . . then . . .') reasoning. In the absence of these abilities, students would be lost in college, certainly by the time they reached upper division undergraduate courses.

Many students, of course, appear on campus lacking formal operational skills, and they may develop them while there. When Young Adults develop these skills on campus, it is impossible to know how neurological maturation, the demands of studying, and social experience each contributed to these gains (Papalia, Olds, and Feldman 1989).

However, formal operational thinking is not always sufficient for successful collegiate experience. This is because students find reality is often neither trustworthy nor dependable. They find, for example, that equally admirable professors present different interpretations of the same phenomenon, and the professors present their views with the same degree of commitment. Students also find that explanations which work at one time and place fail on other occasions, and so they come to learn that reality appears to change with context. *Charles (YA,U)* described competing views when he talked about the diversity of perspectives he encountered on beginning college. 'Say in my residence hall', he began, 'my roommate lived on a farm near a really small town in western North Dakota which might as well be a different planet from the world that I've grown up in'. To students going to college to learn from experts about the world — how it is organized and how it functions — these realizations about the relativity of truth are very unsettling. And the cognitive abilities conferred by formal operational thinking, though powerful, are insufficient to the task of dealing with shifting realities and varying contexts.

Post-Formal Operational Thought

Resolution to this problem is enjoyed by students who reach a post-formal operational level of thinking. They come to see knowledge as being non-absolute and relativistic in nature (Kramer, 1983; Perry, 1970), and adopt dialectic thinking (Basseches, 1980; Kramer and Woodruff, 1986; Labouvie-Vief, 1980; Riegel, 1976) as a way of dealing with that knowledge. More specifically, they see reality as presenting much data of all kinds, and mounting an argument means choosing from among those data available only the information supporting the positions being advocated. Proponents carefully choose whatever perspectives, opinions, and facts support their thesis and attack opposing views; opponents do the same thing, carefully selecting the support for their position, the antithesis (Basseches, 1980). In other words, post-formal operational thinkers are genuinely able to accept the fact that persons on different sides of an issue see things differently.

And they are not surprised if, through discussion, the adversaries reach a synthesis, a new view of reality which is acceptable to all. Neither are post-formal operational thinkers surprised if the combatants fail to reach any agreement at all; the antagonists have simply appeared and presented their differing views of reality without either changing themselves or the people who heard them. Perry (1970) notes that to people lacking the ability to accept the notion of different realities for different people, the kinds of conversations just described are not only impossible to understand, they are most unsettling.

Amber (A,P) described the way a student who has not reached post-formal operations responds to a professor whose teaching required post-formal operational thought. 'They want you to find it', she said, 'but it's more . . . it's a game — "I know it and you're going to have to figure it out and I'm not going to tell you"'. Apparently, Amber has not yet come to grips with the idea that 'it' exists in the mind of the protagonist, and that another advocate will argue equally compellingly for a different 'it'.

Much of the following description of cognitive development is based on the work of Perry (1970). However, there is great diversity of opinion in the literature concerning the acquisition of post-formal operations. Theoretical papers attempt to define or conceptualize post-formal operations (Kramer, 1983; Riegel, 1976; Leadbeater, 1986; Labouvie-Vief, 1980) while others report empirical studies of the nature, prerequisites, and assessment of post formal operational thought (Cropper, Meck and Ash, 1977; Commons, Richards and Kuhn, 1982; Kramer and Woodruff, 1986; Basseches, 1980; Perry, 1970).

According to Perry (1970), people move from formal operations to post-formal operations in response to a variety of influences including the environment they live in and the teachers with whom they work. The process follows identifiable stages with resolution of the tasks of one stage a necessary condition for successful resolution of subsequent stages. Perry (1970) asserts that each stage reflects the development not only of cognition, but also of identity and morality. The stages themselves will not be described here (see Perry for a complete description); we will, however, discuss attributes of these stages.

Prime among these attributes is a set of rules, a set of values, perhaps, for viewing the environment in which one lives and selecting from it that subset of data one needs in order to interact with others successfully. Having recognized that the real world is a complex place, people emerging into adulthood must find ways of choosing attributes to attend to (and so identify attributes to ignore) in approaching and solving the problems they face. This is most commonly done by making a commitment to something, and it is the rules and values arising from such a commitment that people use to organize the world and examine it in a structured and understandable way.

Concerning this commitment, Erikson observes that, 'I would . . . claim that we [humans] have almost an instinct for fidelity — meaning that when you reach a certain age you can and must learn to be faithful to some ideological view' (as quoted by Evans, 1967, p. 30). In essence, Erikson is saying that the need to make the commitment is universal, but that the object of that commitment is up to each person. Thus the commitment may arise from any number of sources. It may be religious, for example, or it may be the decision to take on a career; in either case, the world view adopted helps the person make sense out of what is otherwise chaotic.

Now in contrast to decisions made by teenagers (where individuals are heavily influenced by peers) the adult decision to commit is made individually. Both the seriousness of the decision and the fact that it is made individually means people 'go out on a limb' when they commit; they risk making mistakes and exposing their ignorance. But they do it because, in return for adopting the values, the views, and the perspective the commitment offers, they take on a way of organizing and making sense of reality. What is more, they can use the perspective they've taken on as a reference point for recognizing and understanding the perspectives used by others to accomplish the same ends (Dusek *et al.*, 1986).

Later in this chapter, we will discuss the ways in which making a commitment also contributes to an aspect of identity development.

Implications for Teachers

People reading this book have all experienced the kind of commitment which Perry (1970) described as required to realize a post-formal operations level of thought. And anyone who has done that can recall the difficulties and insecurities associated with the decision. Do I want to be a doctor? a teacher? an accountant? Though the decision sounded like a professional one, its implications were more far reaching than that, and we knew it. It was not a decision made easily; it was a decision fraught with concerns. And this leads to the first implication for teachers: People at this point — regardless of their chronological ages — show reduced self-assurance during the period between realizing the world is a relativistic place and becoming comfortable with the outcomes of the commitment they have made. This means not only that teachers must be emotionally supportive, but that they should also provide instructional activities appropriate to these students' needs.

This might mean presenting conflicting data and involving students in a dialectic discussion of it. Such a discussion would also need to consider moral issues since questions of values are part and parcel of post formal operational thought. This also means that the students would need to enjoy the emotional support of the teacher as they considered these issues — issues which were potentially foreign and/or difficult for them. Finally, instruction of this variety provides people at the point of making their commitments with opportunities to both consider important questions and hear how others are addressing them.

The second implication concerns teachers as role models. Teachers need to demonstrate, through their own behavior, that it is possible to live with the uncertainty in the world, and they also need to show how they — as members of the profession they are role-modeling — deal with the issues that face them. Perry notes that teachers can do this by being open and allowing students to see that educators themselves experience doubt and uncertainty, but that they work with it and then through it. Teachers show that difficult issues, though daunting, can be approached and, often, handled. What is more, teachers show that doing this can be understandable and enjoyable. We can all remember watching a favorite professor lead a class and thinking, 'That must be what it's like to be a doctor or lawyer or an engineer or a teacher.' In invoking that kind of imagery, we 'tried on' feeling what it must be like to be a member of that profession.

College teachers show that there are ways to successfully deal with an otherwise uncertain world. For example, *Robert (A,P)* described the best teacher he encountered in college by saying,

> I guess I'm thinking of one in particular right now who was an extremely brilliant man but at the same time was very compassionate with students . . . He would always — rather than giving the answers or explaining how he thought about something — he would always try to pull the student forward a little bit from where they were at. And so he would always seek to find out what the student was thinking. If they were dealing with a particular idea in class he would ask [the] student, 'How does that fit with your experience? How does that fit with your understanding of reality? Does that seem true to you? Don't accept this because it's in the book or because someone requires you to say this . . . . And then, where can you go from here? How can you think about things, let's see how you're thinking about things now and let's see where you can go from there. Are there other ways of thinking that you haven't discovered yet or haven't considered and let's investigate some of those. And what are the implications of the way you're thinking?'

In other words, *Robert's* professor was accepting of the students' uncertainties and incompletely developed abilities. By turning their questions back to them, he evidenced confidence in them and told them it was all right — indeed, it was important — to ask the questions they were asking. And what is most important was that he was a role model of how people in his profession could work with others.

Notice the difference between *Robert's (A,P)* and *Amber's (A,P)* descriptions of professors who do not furnish 'right' answers. *Robert* sees this as evidence of a fine teacher while *Amber* seems to regard it as spitefulness of a sort. Their perceptions are influenced by their stage of development. *Robert* understands the relativistic thought which frustrates *Amber*.

Along with role modeling, teachers need to provide support to students, and the nature of the support depends on how far along students are in their thinking about making a commitment. Persons at early stages (e.g., undergraduates, perhaps, regardless of age) need reassurance and need to be shown what people are like who have made commitments of various kinds. Since these students are questioning themselves, they need to be validated as people: They need to know that their search is an important one and, even though they must make their decisions alone, that there are people available to be empathic, to counsel, and to help. According to Perry, they need a sense of community to help give them the courage to take the risks necessary for working out commitment. *Daniel (YA,G)* summarized it very nicely when he said, 'Alone as an undergraduate can be pretty scary'.

This kind of aloneness calls for the kinds of group instructional activities mentioned earlier. *Steve (A,G)* commented on this when he said,

> I think . . . the undergraduate student perceives a group as being a safer thing, rather than being based just on his interpretation and writing skills and so forth. If you're in a group . . . it's the group consensus that writes the report or whatever — not [an] individual expression of what [a person] feels the situation is.

Later, when people have made their commitments, the kind of faculty support appropriate to and necessary for them changes. We are talking now about Graduate and some Professional students, people who now need to study the ways in which other people who have made the same commitment they've made deal with doubt and uncertainty, and how those people resolve problems in the process. The nature of the role model, in other words, is different; while, for the undergraduate, the role model said, 'People like me have ways of handling these problems successfully'. The role model now says, 'Here are the ways people like you and me can approach these problems' and offers both examples and instructional experiences. The focus, in other words, is more squarely on the subject matter taught and less on the person doing the teaching.

Thus, the uncommitted student watches the teacher to see if he would like to be like her in the ways she approaches the world and solves the problems it presents ('I'm uncertain about myself just now', an uncommitted student might say, 'and I wonder whether being like her will make my life better'.) The graduate or professional student, on the other hand, has already made her commitment and is looking to the professor to show her how to do the things she's decided she wants to do ('I know what I want' she says, 'I'm looking to him to show me how to do it').

Jerry (A,P) reflected on his life now that he has made his commitment. 'I think I'm much more self-assured', he observed in reflecting on how becoming comfortable with this commitment to be a lawyer changed the way he felt about himself. Then, indicating that he was learning some of the ways lawyers approach their world, he noted, 'You simply can't rely on anybody else in law school to get by, because . . . it's how *you* interpret something'. He had made his decision, and now he's turning to the law faculty to help him implement what he's decided to do.

Stages in Becoming a Post-Formal Operations Thinker

There are stages in the process of moving beyond formal operational thought (Perry, 1970). While early stages begin with a search for the 'right' or 'correct' view of something, students evidence a weakening of the belief that such a 'right' or 'correct' answer exists, and ultimately come to the view that there is a diversity of opinions. This is troubling and unsettling to them — especially since many of them arrived on campus to learn about truth from the experts they found there.

Intermediate stages in development have the student seeing knowledge and values as relativistic with the question that has a right or wrong answer being a special case of what 'they' (the faculty) want. What is important here is both the students' acknowledgement of the relativity of reality and the conclusion growing from that acknowledgement that a commitment — embodying a way to view the world — is necessary. That commitment, of course, provides students with a world view that simplifies things by allowing them to focus on certain aspects of reality, ignore others, and do it all with reference to the set of values coming with the commitment. And so each student who becomes a post formal operational thinker commits.

The latter stages of this process involve students experiencing the consequences of their commitments. They explore stylistic issues (how does it feel to live one's life making decisions using the value system provided by the commitment) as well as the responsibilities taken on (how does it feel to do the things one does having made this commitment).

People in the latter stages realize an affirmation due to having made their commitments, an affirmation arising from their commitments and becoming a part of their identities. *Daniel (YA,G)*, during his second year of aerospace studies, says 'I can really, just in this last semester, even, really see where I'll probably fit into the grand scheme of things. I have a purpose'. The student, in short, sees the commitment as an unfolding, ongoing activity through which he expresses his lifestyle.

Final Notes on Post-Formal Operational Thought

Making a commitment leading to a student's developing post-formal thought can occur in Adults as well as Young Adults; because this decision is also a career decision, it is not strictly the domain of 18 to 24 year olds. Thus when any student commits, he has made a career decision, a decision that implies learning to think like a lawyer, or an engineer, or a nurse, or whatever it is the student elects. In other words, the development of thought is intimately related to the commitment to a career which is intimately related to the knowledge of who one is. Erikson summarizes this nicely saying:

> Such cognitive orientation forms not only a contrast but a complement to the need of the young person to develop a sense of identity, for, from among all possible and imaginable relations, he must make a series of ever-narrowing selections of personal, occupational, sexual, and ideological commitments. (1968, p. 245)

Identity Development

Identity and Cognitive Development

Clearly, students, regardless of age, who achieve post-formal thinking do so and realize changes in their identities in an interdependent manner. Students learn to think like professionals and begin thinking of themselves as professionals about the same time. This is an important shift in one aspect of each student's identity.

It is important for several reasons. As noted earlier, declaring for a profession means adopting the values and morality of the profession. It also means taking on as one's own the profession's way of seeing the world so that the post-formal thinker uses the profession's values to sort out the evidence appropriate to the thesis and the antithesis in any given situation.

These skills also make it easier to recognize and understand others with the same world view. It is easier to make the 'like me/not like me' distinction by seeing what sorts of things other people recognize as important in the world, what sorts of things they ignore. It is the combination of values and the application of those values in the world that sets each student — and the group in which the committed student claims membership — apart from other groups.

Kohlberg and Gilligan (1971), Perry (1970), and Waterman (1982) all see recognition of relativism in reality as a transitional stage in moral and identity development. Kohlberg and Gilligan, for example, report that concrete operations (being able to deal with only what is real — a level of cognitive development seen in children aged about 6–12) — is required for conventional morality (do certain things because people will think ill of you if you don't). People with principled or post-conventional morality do the right thing because they have a set of universally applicable principles which guide them. This level of moral reasoning requires formal operational thinking, and so this raises interesting questions about the relationships among thinking, questioning conventional morality, and identity: Seeing the world as a place where nothing is certain undermines the notions of the certainties of conventional morality. Seeing the world relativistically requires both more sophisticated thinking and the adoption of a morality which allows one to function successfully.

Stages in Identity Development

Identity development is a lifelong process (Waterman, 1982). Though it is minimal in high school (where the major source of identity for a person is a group of friends), there is much identity development in college. College confronts students with a variety of views of life and opportunities for commitment, and these confrontations and opportunities may help students address their identities (indeed, college students are prime candidates for identity crises).

As we've noted already, identity development — especially as it relates to choice of careers — is not limited to the Young Adults on campus. Giese (1988) reports that much career change takes place among the adult population; people change careers throughout adulthood for reasons ranging from boredom, failure, and lack of fulfillment through the desire to clarify one's goals in life. All of these were reflected in *Robert's (A,P)* decision to leave the ministry and become a physician. He felt he needed to know more, to do more, and he was influenced in his decision by the personal experience of the untimely loss of a member of his family through illness.

Note, though, that *Robert* did not change his profession abruptly. Indeed, changes in identity, like cognitive development, follow stages (e.g., see *Marcia*, quoted in Waterman, 1982). *Foreclosure* is the stage where people have pseudo-identities, often based on choices made for them by others such as parents. This is the stage preceding an identity crisis (which Erikson sees as mild and occurring over a period of time and resulting in a new sense of who one is). *Billie Jo (YA,U)* exemplified foreclosure in her responses to a question on whether going to college had changed her values. 'I don't think so', she said, adding 'It [college] has narrowed them. I have grown up with these same basic values that I have now. Just pretty traditional . . . I think what college has done for me more than anything has cemented [them]'.

The next stage, *identity diffusion*, comes after a person has an identity crisis and has not yet resolved that crisis. This is followed by *moratorium*, a stage when the student is in the process of trying out various occupations/ideologies but has not yet made a commitment. *Jerry (A,P)* described moratorium very nicely:

> I think [I was] a pretty typical teenager . . . wasn't quite sure what I wanted to do. The same with [being an] undergrad — I pursued two or three different courses of study. I had gotten quite a few scholarships to go into chemical engineering so that's what I started in. It didn't take me long to realize that wasn't what I wanted to study. So I really experimented doing some different things that I wanted to do. I spent five years getting through undergrad even though I CLEPPED [tested out of] thirty-five hours before I started.

Identity achievement is the final stage, it is the point where each student has made a commitment. The decision was their own, it was made freely, and they are now in the process of realizing the implications of that commitment. Not surprisingly, identity achievement increases with the experience of going to college (Waterman, 1982). Indeed, Waterman argues that students undergoing an identity crisis in college are in a good position to see their ways through to a successful resolution. However, success at identity achievement is uneven; it is most stable in vocational areas, least stable in religion and politics.

Finally, identity development does not stop with graduation from college. Rather, finding employment and working in the area of one's choice means further experience with the set of moral values taken on in college and increased experience in using the world view adopted in solving the problems one faces. And, lastly, working as a professional cements one's identity as a member of that profession.

It seems clear that, because cognitive development and identity development are related processes, the stages of each should be related. It's equally clear, though, that both the process of becoming a post-formal operation thinker and moving from foreclosure to identity achievement are gradual processes with their respective stages appearing together or not appearing together depending on the individual.

Implications for Teaching

Because becoming a member of a profession implies a change in identity as well as learning the skills expected of members of the profession, it is good for teachers to cast problems for students in ways that will let them begin thinking of themselves as professionals. Rather than asking an education student to develop a lesson plan, it is better to tell him 'you are a seventh grade teacher, and you need to develop a lesson plan dealing with magnetism' as a way of getting started. Then, when the project is complete, have the student present the lesson plan to other students who are also playing roles as 'teachers' as well as someone representing the school's 'administration'. Doing things in this way will help students become comfortable with the idea that they can see themselves as the professionals they want to be. Imagery is a very powerful tool in teaching.

Similarly, it is important to have students discuss the values implicit in implementing what they're learning. And at the same time, they can examine their work from the points of view of others with whom they might work. In a malpractice case in moot court, for example, it might be useful to have the law students representing the different sides attempt to see their work from the perspectives of the physicians involved in the case. The goal here is *not* to establish right or wrong or culpability or responsibility or any other of the issues discussed in the moot court case; rather, the goal of the discussion is to discover the perspective of each of the interested parties in order to understand how the evidence they present reflects the perspective that came with the commitment they'd made in taking on a career.

In other words, the idea behind these kinds of activities is simply that making a professional commitment is a way people have of providing themselves with a perspective on an otherwise exceedingly complex world. The idea driving the activities is that different professions adopt different perspectives, and the activities simultaneously allow students to view each and to practice trying it on. Teachers, in these cases, both provide students with opportunities they wouldn't otherwise have, and provide support to students in the tentative steps they take in the trying on process.

Part II

Our Study and Its Findings

Introduction

The pages which follow present information on Adult Learners which, to our knowledge, has not been examined through a comprehensive study. These pages also rely on the previous two chapters; these pages use the information on adult development and adult learners in interpreting the results of our study. The data we collected and the interpretive perspectives provided by the chapters on Adult learners and adult development allowed us to understand Adults' learning needs and consider approaches to teaching Adults.

Chapter 3 ('Our study, our students') briefly describes the study we mounted. The purpose of that description is an outline of how we developed our survey instrument, how we defined our population and selected our sample, the analytic strategy we chose to extract information from the data, and the procedures we used to interpret those findings. Since interviews with the thirteen people introduced earlier were an important aspect of the interpretation, we describe those Young Adults and Adults in more detail here. Chapter 3 also provides information on the University of North Dakota. We offer this information because some readers will find it useful in (i) satisfying themselves that results of this study are generalizable to institutions of higher education elsewhere, and (ii) identifying specific ways in which findings reported here apply to their schools, their students. For these reasons, we describe both the University and its student population. We also discuss ways in which our findings generally compare with those of other studies. Comparison of our findings with those of other researchers is, of course, a major theme in Chapters 4 and 5.

Chapter 4 ('Issues related to college attendance') describes topics such as time utilization and reasons for attending college, topics impacting on, but not a part of, the teaching and learning experiences of Adults. Like Chapter 2, it ends with a consideration of educational implications.

Chapter 5 ('Issues related to teaching and learning') is the second of our 'findings' chapters. This chapter indeed considers topics describing things taking place in the classroom and other settings where learning occurs. We talk about a variety of findings ranging from obstacles Adults face in attending the university to preferred instructional styles to descriptions of best and worst teachers. This chapter also ends with implications for teachers.

Arguably the most interesting of our findings is something that appears only rarely in the findings of our study: Statistical evidence of an interaction between students' ages and colleges (Undergraduate, Graduate, and Professional). This means two related things. First, Adult students in any of the three colleges share attributes with Adults in the other two just as findings for any given college apply to all students in that college regardless of age. Second, only rarely did we encounter something unique to students of a particular age enrolled in a particular college. One example of this was our finding that Young Adult Undergraduates preferred group instructional methods far more than we'd expected simply knowing they were Young Adults and Undergraduates. This was an interaction because the combination of Age and College was associated with an outcome not anticipated given knowledge of Age and College.

This means, for example, that Adult Undergraduates, though a large and important group on campus, are not unique. They can be described in terms of attributes of Adults (which they share with Adult Graduate and Adult Professional students), and attributes of Undergraduates (which they share with Young Adult Undergraduates).

A second major finding is the extraordinary way in which cognitive and identity development issues bear on both interpretation of our findings and derivation of educational implications. For example, our findings show that all Undergraduates, regardless of whether they are Young Adults or Adults, look to faculty to validate them as people. While this is easy to understand for Young Adults (they are insecure because they have not yet finished separating themselves from their families of origin), the explanation is less clear for Adults (because they have already finished that task). We argue here that Adult Undergraduates look for validation of themselves as people because they have not yet reached identity achievement which comes from becoming comfortable with making a commitment — to a career, for example. The resulting insecurity causes them to look for the same things from teachers as the Young Adults with whom they share their classes. One educational implication bearing on this Undergraduate need is the teacher's making certain she is available to students because while she is 'officially' answering their questions, by being available to them she is also speaking to them about the fact that she values them as people.

Chapter 6 ('Recommendations for teaching adult students') takes the implications from Chapters 1–5 and integrates them into a series of thirteen specific recommendations. These are described both from the perspective of how they are justified and what needs to be done to implement them. In the former case, justification comes from the data themselves and from the background information presented in Chapters 1 and 2; in the latter case, implementation is described through specific techniques teachers of Adult students might use.

Chapter 7 ('Epilogue and summary') is our last chapter. In it, we report what we've found about our thirteen Young Adult and Adult students three years after we completed our study and, in this sense, it is an epilogue. It is a summary because what we've learned turned out to be readily explainable from the findings of this study as reported in Chapters 5 and 6. We feel very good about what we learned from following up on our students; in addition to allowing us an independent observation that our findings were generalizable beyond the circumstances under which we collected our data, it was good to learn that these people were doing well.

Chapter 3

Our Study, Our Students

Methodology

As we noted in the Preface, we mounted this study to provide an integrated picture of Adult learners. Toward that end, we surveyed Young Adult and Adult full-time students on campus using methods which are described in detail in Appendix A. In addition, we sketch our methodology here in detail sufficient for understanding the results presented in the following chapters.

We elected to do a survey in order to collect information data from people representing the range of students on campus. Since we expected some of what we learned would be related to the attributes of age and the point each student was at in their academic careers, we used a stratified random sampling with age (Young Adult and Adult) and college (Undergraduate, Graduate and Professional) as the stratifying variables. We drew samples of about one hundred students from each of the six strata (Age and College combinations), a number we selected because, assuming a response rate of 50 per cent, we would be able to declare a difference of 10 per cent between two groups to be statistically significant at alpha = 0.05. However, this was our 'worst case scenario'; we really expected a higher response rate and, in anticipation of that, we planned to continue looking for 10 per cent differences, but we could declare them significant at a more rigorous alpha level.

In keeping with our goal of providing a broad picture of Adult learners, our questionnaire covered issues ranging from why students attended through perceptions of instruction and teachers. In other words, not only did we want to be able to describe the population of interest to us, we wanted to describe it across the entire spectrum of educational issues associated with attending college.

Using procedures described in Appendix A, we received usable questionnaires from 69 per cent of the people in our sample, a response rate, we felt, that was high enough to protect the external validity of our study. Then, using multi variate of variance analysis with the quantitative data and simple content analysis methods for the responses to open ended questions (again, see Appendix A), we completed our analysis and began interpreting the results produced.

Because of the healthy response rate, we were able to declare a difference of 10 per cent between two groups (e.g., Young Adult Undergraduates and Adult Undergraduates) statistically significant at alpha = 0.01. Thus, in the sequel, any time statistical significance is reported, readers can consider there is less than one chance in a hundred that differences between two groups as large as 10 per cent could be found on the basis of chance alone. We also elected not to report values of test statistics (always F-ratios) since (i) our sample sizes were large enough to detect differences we considered to be important, (ii) our use of a rigorous alpha level meant the likelihood of type I (false positive) findings was adequately controlled in spite of the large number of hypotheses tested; and (iii) including them within the context of summary tables would add considerably to the length of this volume. Readers wishing to see the actual values of the test statistics should be in touch with us; we will be happy to share them.

Though we did no conventional statistical tests with our data from open ended questions, we nevertheless looked for differences of 10 per cent between two groups and, when we found them, considered them to be 'significant' as well.

We interpreted all our findings by looking to see (i) whether results were consistent with one another; (ii) whether they were consistent with the literature; and (iii) if they are squared with the expectations of Young Adult and Adult learners from the Undergraduate, Graduate, and Professional colleges surveyed. To do this, we interviewed the thirteen Young Adults and Adults sketched in the preceding pages and described in more detail later in this chapter. Specifically, we presented them with findings of our study and asked them for their interpretations and whether there were events in their lives bearing on the findings as they understood them. The quotes enriching the prose in this book came from those interviews.

We chose this methodology because it allowed us to collect data and reach conclusions unavailable through the use of narrower approaches. These data and conclusions concern differences across groups (such as Colleges) as well as identifying variation within groups (such as Adults). We describe those findings in the next two chapters.

And so we developed a survey instrument, selected a sample, collected data, analyzed it, and interpreted those results produced. An important remaining question, though, is whether those findings are descriptive of Adult learners beyond our campus, and it is to that issue that we now turn.

Students at the University of North Dakota (UND)

Eric Sevareid, who was born in Velva, North Dakota, once observed that his home state was a void in the American consciousness. People just don't know much about North Dakota. Although this is more of a problem for the state tourism board than it is for us, we know that people interested in adult learners will examine our findings asking how they apply to their students, their universities. Since this is really a question of how the population of adult learners at the University of North Dakota (UND) compares to similar populations elsewhere, we present two kinds of information as an aid in putting our adult learners in perspective. The first is largely demographic and considers issues such as the characteristics of full-time UND students while the second deals with attributes of adult learners, the attributes we looked at in doing the study reported here. We begin with the demographic issues.

The University

Like many other states, North Dakota has a state university system. The University of North Dakota, with its main campus in Grand Forks, is the research institution in the system chiefly responsible for educating the state's citizens in the liberal arts and the professions (North Dakota State University, in Fargo, is a land grant school which also does research, though its thrust is agricultural).

UND is easily recognizable to people familiar with state schools. It has a traditional variety of programs (sciences, the humanities, education, engineering, and law and medicine) as well as a more recently opened Center for Aerospace Sciences. Its faculty is made up of scholars educated at universities from across the country and around the world, scholars who compete successfully for grant monies, do research and perform other creative activities, and publish in refereed journals and present at national and international meetings. As is the case at other universities in the United States, the majority of our faculty are tenured.

Many of our faculty teach in our graduate programs in the arts, the sciences, the humanities, education, and other areas, and our graduates take positions in the state, in the region, and elsewhere around the country. These positions range from the private sector to public service — including education at all levels. We have, especially in recent years, enjoyed a large number of foreign students so that our instructional and research efforts are increasingly represented around the world.

Student Body Size

In recent years, the University of North Dakota enrolled about 11,000 students each year in its undergraduate, graduate, and law and medical

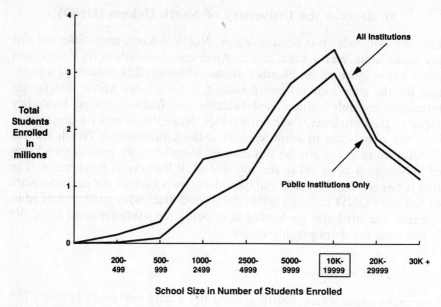

Figure 1: Total enrollment in higher education of students in the US for institutions of different sizes

programs. On average, this is about 35 per cent of all students attending college full-time in the state (based on figures from Snyder and Hoffman, 1991). In terms of enrollment, UND is in the 10,000–19,999 student body size, the modal college and university size category according to the National Center for Educational Statistics (Snyder and Hoffman, 1991). The fact that schools of UND's size are at the middle of the distribution (see Figure 1) means that we are average (i.e., typical) in this regard. Middle-sized colleges like UND, taken together, may well be the workhorses of American higher education: They educate more students than any other size institution in the United States, and, indeed, public schools of the 10,000–19,999 size enrolled more students in 1988 (2.9 million) than did all private schools in this country regardless of their size (2.8 million).

In other words, UND is typical of colleges and universities in its enrollment. We make this claim because it is middling in size, and because schools of UND's size educate more students than another group of institutions.

Demographics

The University of North Dakota is also typical in terms of its population of full-time students. For example, when students are divided according to Age and College, the percentages of students in each of the six groups created mirror well the corresponding national percentages (see Table 1).

Table 1:   Student profiles at UND and nationally

Student Group	University of North Dakota		United States
	Number of Students	Percentage	Percentage
Age Breakdown			
24 and under	8134	73.91	80.52
25 and older	2870	26.09	19.48
Total	11005*	100.00	100.00
Gender Breakdown			
Male	5738	52.14	50.56
Female	5267	47.86	49.44
Total	11005*	100.00	100.00
College Breakdown			
Undergraduate	9551	85.42	86.52
Graduate	1223	10.94	11.37
Professional	407	3.64	2.10
Total	11181**	100.00	100.00

*   On-campus students only.
** All students enrolled on-campus and off-campus.
Source: Percentages for the United States come from Synder and Hoffman, 1991.

Clearly, UND students are generally typical of higher education students in the United States in terms of the percentages enrolled as Undergraduate, Graduate, and Professional students, while the percentages of male and Adult students are a little higher than the corresponding national figures. There are two explanations for this situation, one due to chance, the other more intimately related to the nature of Adult learners. First, our figures may simply reflect the considerable heterogeneity in the population of higher education students generally, and Adult learners in particular (see Knox, 1980). In other words, the fact that our percentages of male and Adult students are a bit above the national average may simply reflect that variability and means nothing more than, on the basis of chance alone, we have a few more males and Adult students. The implication of this argument is that other schools elsewhere have a few less.

The second and more theory-based explanation is that these numbers in fact reflect an important attribute of Adult learners. Specifically, and as we will show later in this book, Adult learners often return to school following important and frequently negative events in their lives. And since the economy of North Dakota has been weak for the past decade, we suspect many North Dakotans (like *Jerry [A,P]*) have experienced such events. Agriculture, the state's chief source of income, is in particular trouble, and the petroleum industry important in the west end of the state has been depressed since the early 1980s. These facts imply that a larger number of adults in our state have faced layoffs, small business failures, farm foreclosures, and the like, and that some percentage of them may have returned to school — a percentage higher than would be the case had the state's economy been better. In other words, rather than implying that

Adults at the University of North Dakota are somehow atypical, these numbers simply reflect realities in the lives of people who become Adult learners.

Most UND students come from middle class backgrounds and grew up in small cities, towns, and rural areas since there are no truly large cities in the state. They tend to come from the state, and, in decreasing frequency, from the region (Minnesota, South Dakota, and Montana), and all other states. As noted earlier, an important percentage of our students also come from foreign countries.

In short, our student body looks very much like what one would expect of an American university.

Adult Learners at the University of North Dakota

We turn now to more personal concerns in the lives and education of the students our university serves. Because knowing about numbers of students describes similarities in broad strokes, we want to show how our Adults are like those in other studies in terms of these kinds of attributes to underscore the point that Adults at UND are, indeed, typical of Adults elsewhere. In doing this, we consider attributes ranging from the psychological to those describing how students feel about their educations.

We begin with the psychological attributes. All adults, whether attending college or not, address similar developmental tasks in the process of working through the same developmental stages. This means that, by virtue of being human beings, we expect our Adults to be just like others elsewhere.

But, of course, not all Adults attend college, and so it is appropriate to look at how ours compare to the subpopulation of Adults who do. They display the same developmental attributes (e.g., many reach a post-formal operations level of thinking) and the issues they dealt with when they enrolled are similar to those identified by other researchers. Our Adults, for example, have approached barriers described by other returning students (see, for example, Darkenwald and Merriam, 1982; Scanlan and Darkenwald, 1984; Cross, 1981; Carp, Peterson and Roelfs, 1974; and Rubenson, 1977). As we will show in the next chapter, these included issues ranging from economics (such as financing schooling) to emotional (such as dealing with self-doubt).

In Chapter 5, we describe how UND Adults also overcame these barriers for reasons recognized by writers working with their own samples of Adults (e.g., Knox, 1977; Aslanian and Brickell, 1980). Our students sought to take on a first profession (most easily seen among Undergraduates and Professional students and described in Chapter 4), and advancing in their careers (more often seen in Graduate students). In this regard, our Adults are like those elsewhere.

Another important similarity between UND Adults and Adults described in the literature is time utilization which is considered in Chapter 4. Our Adults report the same difficulties of balancing all the responsibilities associated with being an Adult, difficulties reported by other researchers (see Cross, 1981).

And all students, regardless of age, have feelings about both what and how they learn. In these regards, UND students are similar to others in the ways they view instructional and evaluation formats (see Even, 1987, for example, for a discussion of Adults' preferred learning styles and Chapter 5 for a consideration of how UND students feel about these issues). Similarly, UND Adults' descriptions of best liked and least liked teachers are comparable to those of other students reported in the literature (e.g., Ross-Gordon, 1991; Alciatore and Alciatore, 1979).

In other words, the results of our study are, in many ways, confirming the results reported by others even though our methodology was different than that employed by other researchers. We take this to mean that Adults at UND are representative of Adult learners on other campuses.

Summary

The University of North Dakota is like many other colleges and universities in the United States. It is like them both in size and in the composition of its student body. It is for this reason that we believe our findings are applicable to other universities.

A Group of Young Adult and Adult Learners

Thus far, we have discussed Young Adult and Adult learners as groups of people with reference to particular individuals to make specific points. Those individuals were part of the group of thirteen Young Adults and Adults whose names appear just after the Preface. We now describe them in more detail in anticipation of using information they provided in their interviews in the course of presenting the results of our study.

In describing these students in detail, we will not share everything we learned about each student. Some of what they told us was not germane to goals of this book, of course, and other things were sufficiently similar to what we learned from other people that repetition would serve no useful purpose. Indeed, in describing each person, we identify those attributes of Young Adults and Adults which come through most clearly for them.

Adults

Adults, as a group, are well described by Overstreet's concept of a *mature person*:

The mature person is not one who has come to a certain level of achievement and stopped there. He is rather a maturing person — one whose linkages with life are constantly becoming stronger and richer because his attitudes are such as to encourage their growth. . . . A mature person, for example is not one who knows a large number of facts. Rather, he is one whose mental habits are such that he grows in knowledge and the wise use of it. (Cited in Knowles, 1980, p. 29)

Jerry, at age 31 and in his last year of law school, is such a person. Prior to attending law school, *Jerry* worked as a laborer in the western North Dakota oil fields, deciding to return to school when oil prices declined. In this regard, *Jerry* is not unusual: Many Adults return to school because of changes (transitions) in their lives (Apps, 1981; Snoddy and Levine, 1986; Tough, 1981) though seldom is there a single reason why adults return to college (Apps, 1981).

Jerry is also quite busy. Besides school work, he does independent research for private attorneys and the state bar association, and he shares custody of a toddler with his former wife. (He attributes his recent divorce, in part, to the rigors of law school).

Robert is a 35-year-old medical student who, like *Jerry*, has returned to school with much experience behind him as well as ongoing family responsibilities. *Robert* is an ordained minister who is also married and has two young daughters. A third child died during the past year after a prolonged illness, and experiences he and his family had with health care professionals during his child's illness renewed his interest in medicine and convinced him that he could best serve the community as a physician. Previously, *Robert* had worked fulltime in a parish in Minnesota, parttime as a night auditor in a motel and at a sports arena, and as a salesman. He now works on an interim basis in churches in the area.

Though *Robert* demonstrates how a life event can motivate Adults to make significant changes in their lives, his motivation is perhaps an even better example of what Knox (1976) refers to as 'the search for meaning' which is, of course, applicable to all Adult learners and not just *Robert*. *Robert* says the manner in which this search was carried on in seminary is a marked contrast to the orientation toward facts and recall he finds in medical school; the search for meaning is present in both places, though it is very different in each.

Amber is a 40-year-old law student who is married and has no children. Prior to attending law school, she had 14 years' experience as a nurse in a variety of settings including working with migrant worker programs in several midwestern states. She currently clerks for a local law firm and is involved in student activities both in the law school and on campus generally.

Although a major change or transition may not be obvious in all

Adult learners, there is often a *need* for change. In *Amber's* case, this need was a feeling that her ability to accomplish the things she wanted to do would be enhanced by a law degree, and that the credibility and respect accompanying a professional degree would be to her advantage as well. *Amber* says her husband had been long involved in academia and is prepared and able to be supportive of the demands made on her by law school. She says this allows her to approach an otherwise demanding program with considerable equanimity.

The important theme of family support in the lives of Adult learners often takes the form of shared responsibilities — since it is otherwise difficult for the student to handle both school work and the demands of employment and family. Indeed, 'home responsibilities', 'child care', and 'not enough time' were three of the top reasons given by adult students who were unable to attend college (Carp, Peterson, and Roelfs, 1974). All of our Adult participants, with the exception of *Jerry*, identified the importance of family support to the quality of their educational experience.

Unlike the preceding students whose studies are in the professions, *Steve* is a graduate student (in the College of Business and Public Administration). He is 34 years old, married, and has children. He works about seven and a half hours a week as a Graduate Teaching Assistant (GTA) and shares domestic responsibilities with his wife, responsibilities requiring about twenty-five hours a week of his time. This time includes caring for the children all day Friday, on evenings, and weekends.

Steve was a partner in an insurance company in a small community before coming to the university — a major change in his life. Deciding to return to campus after being away from college for a number of years was not a decision lightly taken. Though *Steve* was confident that this was something he wanted to do, he also entertained reservations about being able to succeed. In this regard, he is like many other Adult learners.

Apps (1981) notes that adults returning to college are often unsure of themselves and troubled by poor self-concepts appearing as concerns about being able to succeed in their new environments. Others note that in these circumstances, fulfillment of esteem needs can make the difference between success and failure in their academic pursuits (Fisher, 1981; Ihejieto-Aharanwa, 1986; Van Ness, 1986).

There is also evidence that adults returning to school after a period of absence often feel powerless and alienated. Time does make a difference to them, however, for once they successfully finish one or more college courses, they feel much more confident (Van Ness, 1986). *Steve* — by the time of our interview — had worked through some of these feelings: When asked whether going to college had changed his values, *Steve* said it had not, but that it did change the way he feels about himself. He now feels more confident about his ability to be successful doing something totally different from his past experience. And he added, 'I guess I have more direction, [more] options in my life than I had before'. In a word, he felt more powerful.

Marlys is a 25-year-old psychology graduate student who comes from a small town. She is married, has a baby, and currently works about twenty hours a week as a GTA while spending about forty hours a week at domestic responsibilities. Although she reports that a career in clinical psychology was 'always kind of in the back of my mind', it was only after completing two years at the Air Force Academy that she was certain she wanted to be a psychologist. Her decision to go to school at UND was based on her husband's taking a job in a nearby town. She finds the biggest obstacle to school is 'finding time to study around the baby's schedule' because, as she notes, studying can be done only when the baby is asleep. And so it is no surprise that when asked what could be done to make obtaining an education easier, she replied that university child care not be restricted to daytime hours. *Marlys* says that while her college experience has reinforced the values she already possessed, she does feel that it has changed her as a person. Her analysis is that, 'It has changed me in my family — extended and everything — I'm the only one who has gone to college so I'm sort of different from everyone else but they don't know why. So I tend to believe that I haven't changed but I know that I really have'.

The last two people are undergraduates. *Jimmy* is a high energy 40 year old who retired recently from the military. He thus exemplifies an important reason for returning to school — a change in occupation (Apps, 1981). And he personifies the multiple commitments that characterize most Adult students; they have numerous responsibilities and tight schedules requiring that they sacrifice recreational activities (Hughes, 1983). He and his wife both work full time (he is a night security guard at a sugar beet processing plant) and run a small farm.

However, a crowded schedule does not mean either emotional or social isolation; he enjoys life in general and his undergraduate program of study in particular. This enjoyment extends to the other undergraduates whom *Jimmy* views in a somewhat paternal manner — he reported taking several of them 'under my wing'.

Naomi is a 47-year-old undergraduate who has had varied and interesting life experiences. She and her husband (who is also a student) have one child who is a college freshman at another institution. *Naomi* is the epitome of the term 'continuing education'; her continuing education included living in a mountain cabin in Europe, developing her musical talents, raising animals on a small farm, and an ongoing involvement with children in the community. She is articulate, intelligent, warm, and demonstrates a quiet strength. *Naomi's* academic interests are education and music, and she has returned to college to become an elementary school teacher. Besides being a fulltime student, she accompanies a small town choir and gives piano lessons.

Young Adults

Young Adults contrast markedly with Adults because their youth precludes them from having had many life experiences. They are often aware of this difference between themselves and their older classmates.

Martin is a 23-year-old law student who majored in accounting as an undergraduate and chose to go directly to law school. In addition to his work as a student, he is a clerk with a law firm approximately twenty to twenty-five hours per week. *Martin* feels that one of the greatest obstacles to his work in law school has been his weak writing background. As an accounting major, he was required to write very little, and he now finds he must work hard to reach the level of skill he feels is appropriate for law school. He says he has a great deal of respect for the older students in his class because he sees them having to balance many more demands on their time than he has.

Britt is a 23-year-old medical student who went directly from high school to college and then to medical school. Though she has never worked fulltime, she has held a series of parttime jobs and is now a member of the National Guard (which means one weekend a month and summer commitments). She also reports feeling 'beat' most of the time because of the physical and emotional demands medical school makes on her. She reports feeling, as a young member of her class, that she is at a bit of a disadvantage, and that older students have a definite advantage due to their life experiences. This advantage includes their abilities to 'make connections' between those experiences and things presented in class so that they have a better appreciation of what they are learning.

Rhonda is a 22-year-old graduate student in the Center for Teaching and Learning who works eight hours a week as a graduate teaching assistant. She is married, pregnant with her first child, and spends six to seven hours a week on housework. As an undergraduate, she worked weekends as a house parent at a school for the blind and, after graduating, served as the director of a developmental home. This latter job not only involved too much administrative work for her, but, because her field was special education, she preferred working with children rather than adults. This situation prompted her to return to college where she is specializing in preschool education because her goal, as she described it, is 'trying to help the future'. The major obstacle so far in her current studies is trying to deal with being very sick during her pregnancy.

The kinds of experiences *Rhonda* reports — particularly her learning about the kinds of jobs she likes and dislikes — are precisely those Young Adults are gaining that Adults have in abundance. And *Rhonda*, in the same manner as the Adults, uses these experiences in the process of making decisions concerning her life.

Rhonda does not feel that going to college has changed her values, but she does feel that it has changed her as a person. When asked if she felt different compared to the person she was before attending college, she replied, 'Yes. A good example of that is . . . my only close girlfriend from high school . . . chose not to go on to college and is married and very happy . . . we used to be so alike and we're so very different now'. *Rhonda* also gained satisfaction from the fact that she has been challenged and knows that she has learned.

Daniel, age 23, is a single graduate student who works about twenty-five hours a week at an outside job. Though he claims no domestic responsibilities, he spends around seven hours a week at housework. He is pursuing a Master's degree in aerospace studies, a program of study he chose because he always wanted to work in the aerospace industry. However, fascination with aerospace was *not* the major motivating factor leading to his enrollment in college; when we asked why he is currently enrolled, he said, 'Actually my parents . . . even out of high school my parents stressed . . . college'. Like many people starting college, *Daniel* was at the moratorium stage in identity development. He had not reached the point where he attended college to address his own goals, his own needs.

Daniel enrolled at UND because he is a member of the North Dakota National Guard and must attend college in this state to receive Guard benefits. He plans to continue his education after finishing his Master's degree because he likes college and, as he said, 'I'm in no hurry to get out and spend the rest of my life working'. When asked how going to college affected the way he felt about himself, *Daniel* reported, 'I can really, just in this last semester even, really see where I'll fit into the grand scheme of things. I have a purpose'. We believe this is the perspective of someone who is moving from being a Young Adult to being an Adult.

Charles, a 19-year-old unmarried undergraduate who is majoring in engineering, is also a National Merit Scholar and an Eagle Scout. *Charles* takes his studies very seriously — indeed, he is very committed to his educational and life plans. Charles also works parttime as a computer programmer.

Billie Jo is a 22-year-old unmarried undergraduate in engineering who is looking forward to graduating soon. She is somewhat of an entrepreneur: As an undergraduate, she bought a small house and has rented out a room to help cover expenses, has worked as a freelance house painter, managed a bingo hall, and worked with the Special Olympics. Though *Billie Jo* sees most undergraduates as trying to 'blend in', to be part of the group, she says that this analysis does not describe her. She sees herself as being more independent than most people her age.

Final Observations

We see Young Adults as being in the process of gaining the experiences (and the insights that come from thinking about those experiences) that characterize Adults. We further believe that the combination of these experiences and the developmental tasks appropriate to Adults (which will be considered in the next chapter) provide Adults with the set of needs and beliefs they bring with them to the college classroom. Clearly, the Young Adults are in transition to becoming Adults.

Chapter 4

Issues Related to College Attendance

Time and the Adult Student

Jerry (A,P) observed:

> You simply don't have enough time to do everything. There wasn't
> enough time to study, there wasn't enough time to spend with my
> family, there wasn't enough time to relax. It really comes down
> to trying to prioritize your own needs and the needs of your
> family. When you are a traditional aged student your time is di-
> vided into two things and that's 'study time' and 'party time'.
>   Later, he said, 'Once you've been out and realized what it is
> you want out of life and realize it's gonna take a lot of work to
> obtain those goals . . . I think it's a lot easier to focus and apply
> yourself than when you're younger and haven't gone out there
> and been in the trenches so to speak, out there working and trying
> to get ahead. A lot of people go straight into law school from
> undergraduate and really have no idea of what they're going to be
> facing once they get out. It's a whole different world.'

Competing Priorities

Attending college for the Adult student means the constant challenge of
balancing competing priorities. While this is the challenge, Adults come
prepared with a way to address it. As *Jerry* points out, because most Adult
students have been 'in the trenches,' they have goals they expect to address by going to school and they know how to manage their time in
addressing those goals. In this chapter, we will explore students' reasons
for attending college and their time allocation.

    As we expected, there were significant differences in time utilization
between Young Adult and Adult students. There were no significant dif-

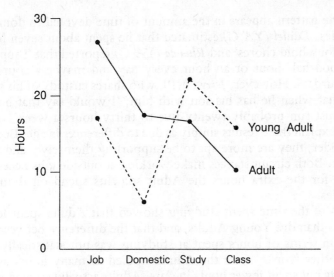

Figure 2: Time allocation for Young Adults and Adults

ferences seen in the way Undergraduates used time as compared to the combined Graduate and Professional students, though Graduate and Professional students did differ significantly from one another in the way they used time. We will first summarize the results and then we will present and discuss the findings in more detail.

We also observed differences between Young Adults and Adults in terms of the reasons they gave for attending college. And while there were no differences between Undergraduates versus the two post-graduate groups in this regard, we did see differences between Graduate and Professional students in why they attended college. We now consider the issues of time utilization and reasons for attending college in more detail.

Allotment of Time

There were significant differences in the time allocation for the two age groups, differences displayed in Figure 2, the diagram showing the number of hours Young Adults and Adults spent at the various activities covered by the questionnaire. The Adult students spent more hours than Young Adults working at outside jobs and domestic responsibilities. This set of circumstances is well-described by Apps (1981) who notes that Young Adults are primarily students while for Adults, the role of student is one among many other roles they play. For example, 40-year-old *Jimmy (A,U)* works thirty-two hours a week as a security guard, week in and week out, while *Billie Jo (YA,U)*, at age 22, reported working ten to fifteen hours a week and noted that the number of hours 'depends on school loads. When it gets tough at school, then [I work] less'.

The same pattern appears in the amount of time devoted to domestic responsibilities. *Daniel (YA,G)* estimated that he spent about seven hours a week 'on household chores' and *Rhonda (YA,G)* reported that 'I suppose I spend a good half hour or an hour every day and maybe a couple of hours on Saturday'. However, *Jerry (A,P)*, who shares custody of his small son, notes that when he has his son with him, 'I would say that housework . . . must run probably twenty-five to thirty hours a week'.

We can explain these results simply as due to differences in age. Because Adults are older, they are more apt to be supporting themselves and their own families. Both circumstances make working at outside jobs necessary and account for the extra hours the Adult students spend on domestic responsibilities.

Analysis of the time spent studying showed that Adults spent fewer hours in class than did Young Adults, and that the difference between the two groups in terms of hours spent at studying was not statistically significant. In other words, since the Adults studied as many hours as the Young Adults but spent fewer hours in class, Adults actually studied more per each class hour than did the Young Adults.

Adults spent about ten hours a week more than the Young Adults on a combination of all four activities: Attending class, studying, attending to housework and children, and outside employment. What is it the younger students do with those ten hours? Given the ages of these students and where they are in their psychological development, we speculate that the time is given over to more social activities. This would be time, then, spent in the company of peers. As noted earlier, *Jerry (A,P)* feels that 'Young Adults' time is divided into two things: "Study time" and "party time"'.

We found no significant differences for Undergraduate time utilization versus the combined Graduate and Professional students, though the time utilization differences between Professional and Graduate students were statistically significant. Time allocations for these two groups are shown in Figure 3.

Specifically, we found no significant differences in the amount of time allotted to domestic responsibilities or studying though Graduate students did spend more time working at outside jobs than did Professional students while Professional students spent more time in class than Graduate students. The Professional students we interviewed confirmed this. For example, *Britt (YA,P)* reported 'with a few exceptions, we're pretty much in class about eight hours a day', and *Robert (A,P)* noted, 'It varies somewhat depending on which [unit of study] we're in . . . but it seems like lately we've been in class from eight to four with maybe an hour off for lunch, but sometimes there's a meeting over lunch hour.' However, *Steve (A,G)* reported fewer hours spent in class, saying, 'I would say I'm in class about fourteen hours [per week]'.

It is likely that allocation of time to class and work simply reflects the

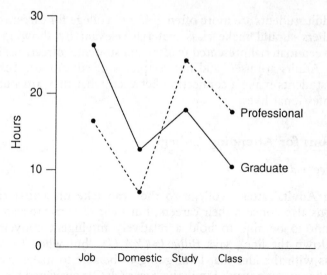

Figure 3: Time allocation for Graduate and Professional students

curricular differences between Graduate and Professional education. In the Professional schools, curriculum is largely lock step and very demanding — students are assigned many hours in class and must be there to do well. In Graduate school, however, assistantships are not only common, but often important mechanisms for professional acculturation and, of course, assistantships qualify as work outside the home. There may well be a Parkinson's law of post-graduate time allocation: Time not allocated to class and family goes to outside employment, and conversely.

Educational Implications

Adult students spend more time dealing with domestic responsibilities and working at outside jobs than do Young Adults. Because of this heavy time commitment, we see a lack of flexibility in Adult students' schedules.

Teachers could simultaneously increase how much Adult students learn and make their lives easier in many ways and this, in turn, will facilitate how much Adults learn. A complete syllabus clearly outlining the semester schedule helps. Further, test dates and due dates for papers or projects should be adhered to since Adult students often rely on babysitters and work schedules and cannot handle unforeseen changes as easily if children and outside employment were not realities in their lives. Because of this, teachers should know that, for Adult students, a canceled class is not the pleasant surprise it is for Young Adults; rather, it can be a great inconvenience since many of them not only have hired babysitters but also have driven long distances to get to class.

Since Adult students are more often going to college for career related reasons, teachers should make class material relevant by showing connections between material presented in class and students' careers (as Knox [1990] notes, Adults are users and not recipients of education). Teachers can help the students make a connection between what they are studying and their professional lives.

Reasons for Attending College

College and Career

Most Young Adults' attend college so they can take on a first career. Adults' reasons also concern their careers, but their reasons are also more varied. 'I want to be able to hold a relatively intelligent conversation somewhere down the line', says *Billie Jo (YA,U)*, 'but when I came to school, it was with the idea that I am going to be able to make my own living and make my own way'. Similarly, *Steve (A,G)* considered his career when he decided to come back to school, though it was with the purpose of taking on a new career. 'I guess [it was] a major career change. My career goal is to teach and do research at the college level . . .'

Adults may be preparing for a first career, a change of career, or career enrichment — but the key word is still 'career'. Given these findings, we question Douvan's (1981) contention that 'Mature students, particularly those in middle age, are often less dominated by vocational preoccupations and are freer to engage in broad areas of curriculum with zest and even passion' (p. 209). Certainly, we see an excitement in Adult students we do not see as often in Young Adults, an excitement that can be described as 'zest and even passion', but it is associated with pursuit of a career.

Figure 4 displays the choices of Young Adult and Adult students. Since each student was asked to choose as many responses as appropriate, the sum of the proportions is more than 1.00. We did this because, as Apps (1981) has noted, Adults usually have multiple reasons for attending college.

Young Adult students overwhelmingly chose 'preparing to begin first occupation' as their reason for attending college. *Billie Jo (YA,U)*, for example, said, 'When I came to school it was with the idea that I'm going to be able to make my own living in my own way', and *Charles (YA,U)* responded that, 'College enables me to do the things I want to do for a career'. These kinds of responses reflect both developmental and chronological issues. Young Adult students are making their career choices — an important event in identity development — and are working toward their first jobs within those careers. With time, they will establish themselves although, as noted, a large percentage of them will change careers at some time in the future.

Adult students are more apt to be attending college because they are

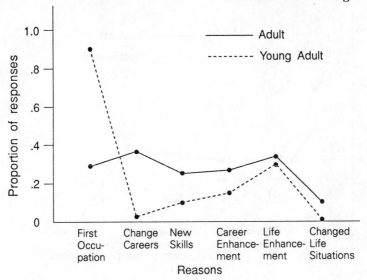

Figure 4: Reasons for attending college for Young Adult and Adult students

changing careers. For example, when we asked *Marlys (A,G)* why she was currently enrolled in college, she said it was because she wanted to be a clinical psychologist, and that, 'It's always been kind of in the back of my mind, but after I left the [Air Force] Academy I started to know for a fact that was what I wanted to do'. *Steve (A,G)*, who had been a partner in an insurance agency for several years, replied, 'I guess [this is] just a major career change. My career goal is to teach and do research at the college level, so getting a Master's degree is the first step towards getting my doctorate.' *Robert (A,P)* described the feelings that motivated him to change careers. 'I needed to know more. I could do more than I was allowed to do in those settings. And I just wouldn't be satisfied if I stayed there for thirty years'.

The intent of Adults to change their careers is not surprising in light of the point we mentioned earlier concerning a sizable proportion of Americans changing their careers for various reasons. Often, these reasons include what Aslanian and Brickell (1980) refer to as 'transitions which involve dilemmas not amenable to problem solving in the usual way'. In other words, Adults change their careers when they face demanding situations which can be handled in no other way. These circumstances might include taking on a job or losing one, getting promoted or passed over for promotion, losing a loved one or increasing the size of the family (Mezirow, 1989).

We also found Adults are more likely to attend college to gain new skills and knowledge to be used in their present occupations and for career enhancement (e.g., taking on new responsibilities in their current jobs). These Adult students may have decided that their careers were well chosen

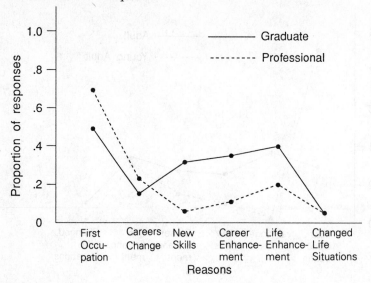

Figure 5: Graduate and Professional students' reasons for attending college

and they wish to do well in them — implying an aspect of a secure adult identity.

We found Young Adults and Adults no different in the proportion reporting life enhancement as a reason for attending college. It is difficult to interpret this result since we did not ask what this term meant to the students. An earlier quote from *Billie Jo (YA,U)*, could be construed as reflecting 'life enhancement'; she said, 'I want to be able to hold a relatively intelligent conversation [some time] down the line'.

Jimmy (A,U) might have been thinking about life enhancement when he said he would like to be well educated and, when asked what that meant, replied, 'To me, being well educated means not only having book knowledge . . . but experience in life itself and common sense and [knowing] how you apply what you're learning to your job and everything'.

Young Adult and Adult students differed in the rates at which they chose change in life situation. It is not surprising that Adults choose this more often since, although 'midlife crises' do not necessarily occur as a developmental passage, there are midlife transitions (Papalia, Olds and Feldman, 1989) such as divorce, retiring from the military, or changes of residence for career reasons (Apps, 1981; Snoddy and Levine, 1986; and Tough, 1981). Such events might cause a person to act upon an already-existing inclination to return to school or require that a return to school be considered. Graduate and Professional students did not differ in their choice of change in life situation.

Figure 5 compares the choices of Graduate and Professional students with respect to reasons for attending college. Professional students more often chose preparing to begin first occupation, possibly because they have completed pre-med or pre-law programs and have aimed for these professions from the start. This was the case with *Martin (YA,P)* who noted, 'I have been a student now since forever, I guess. I never did take any time off between undergraduate and law school'.

We found Professional students also chose 'changing occupation' as a reason more often than did Graduate students; students going to law and medical school are more likely than graduate students to be taking on a new career. This finding led us to wonder whether the opposite was also true — that students attending Graduate school are more likely to be doing so to further their careers in the areas in which they currently work.

Indeed, more Graduate than Professional students chose gaining new skills and knowledge for present occupation. This result may reflect the fact that people in various professions such as teaching, nursing, and counseling often return to college for an advanced degree. For example, teachers might work toward MA's even though they plan no change in their present jobs. It is also worth noting that people in law and medicine who seek advanced education would not have appeared in our sampling frame. Post-graduate medical training is conducted through residency programs which are not run on campus, but rather through affiliated programs.

We also found that more Graduate than Professional students chose career enhancement. We believe this is because professionals such as psychologists, social workers, and chemists may return to graduate school to obtain a PhD, allowing them to advance in their professions.

More Graduate than Professional students chose life enhancement, but again, we wonder how they define that term. It might mean more money, more security, or exposure to new experiences.

Summary

Adult students spent more hours working at outside jobs and on domestic duties than did Young Adult students though the two groups spent about as much time studying. The fact that Adults spent as much time studying even though they carried fewer hours of class implies they prepare more for each class hour. In addition, Young Adult students reported going to college to prepare for their first occupation more often than did Adults.

Adult students spent more time on outside jobs than did Young Adult students and, as might be expected, were more likely to be attending college to change careers, to enhance their present career, or to learn new skills for their work.

Graduate students reported working more hours than did Professional students and took fewer classes while spending about the same amount of time studying. They were more often attending college to gain new skills and enhance current occupations. They were also going to college to enhance their lives.

Chapter 5

Issues Related to Teaching and Learning

Observations of an Adult Learner

Jimmy (A,U) had some observations on how Adults and Young Adults use their time.

> I have had some of the classes that I'm now taking some years ago, 'but due to the experience that I've gained over the last twenty years, I now have a better feeling about who I am. I go into class and sit down with the idea I'm going to learn and will be able to apply what I'm learning. I take this a lot more seriously than does a younger student.
>
> The younger student has a variety of things going at a given time. He feels he's got to take a certain number of courses so he has school work to do, but his social life and his car and various other things are more important than his classes. I've noticed that a lot of younger students might show up once or twice a week for class while the older-than-average student shows up every class and wants to listen to the instructor.

Contemporary Students, Former Students

Students like *Jimmy* are different from those many college teachers remember from the days when they were Undergraduates and the student body was relatively homogeneous. Students generally entered college directly from high school, tended to be between the ages of eighteen and twenty-two, were fulltime students, and usually graduated in four years. In the 1990s and beyond, this student will be the exception rather than the rule. This is because people are now preparing for two or three vocational changes during their lifetimes and may well return to college in anticipation of each of them; women are returning to college after their children are grown; and the rising cost of college tuition requires that students work to partially pay for their tuition so that students take more than four years to graduate. College teachers must ask whether this new student population will require teaching which is different from that used in the past generation, and if the answer is affirmative, what changes should they make to ensure that all the students learn?

In the sections that follow, we will address a variety of teaching and learning issues describing contemporary students. We will report results, identify differences among groups, and end with some suggestions about what these findings mean for faculty at a university enrolling the kinds of students described here.

Preferred Instructional Style

Findings

Our study suggests there are no differences in preferred instructional styles attributable to the different Ages, and in this way agrees with the work of others (e.g., Dubin and Okin, 1983; Mackie, 1981; Even, 1982; Moore, 1982). Individual differences — and not Age — dictated the preferred instructional style although, we note, preferences are colored by the usual teaching methods each student has experienced (e.g., heavier use of lecture in professional colleges, and greater use of laboratories in the sciences and fine arts). These findings also agree with Beder's and Darkenwald's (1982) observation that classroom practices do not vary sharply as a function of age.

In other words, universal prescriptions for instructional methods most appropriate to students of any given Age are ill advised; they ignore the diversity of learning styles found in learners in any Age group. Kasworm (1990) agrees; she concluded from her analysis of 345 studies on Under-graduate Adult students that chronological age is not the key variable. Rather, age reflects certain life and educational experiences, perceptual expectations, and a historical/generational effect, but not preference for learning style.

The failure to find differences in preferred instructional formats does not mean that students value all instructional techniques equally; indeed the opposite is true. We asked respondents to check the teaching methods they most valued, and the results are presented in Table 2.

Scree test results (scree tests are described in Appendix A) indicated four identifiable clusters of techniques; the two most popular (instructional methods 1–3 and 4–9 in Table 2) either involved hands-on activities of some variety or were well known to students. With regard to this last point, Cross (1982) explains Graduate and Professional students' preference for methods, particularly lecture, by observing that:

Table 2: Ratings of instructional methods

Rank	Instructional Method	Mean Rating
1	Practical Projects	.94
2	Lectures with Discussion	.92
3	Use of Simulation	.90
4	Student Participation in Course Design	.85
5	Individual Projects	.80
6	Small Study Group	.78
7	Case Studies	.77
8	Seminars at which Student's Own Relevant Work Experiences Are Discussed	.76
9	Group Projects	.76
10	Computer Assisted Instruction	.72
11	Course Requiring Writing Assignments	.65
12	Analysis of Research Studies	.53
13	Seminars where Student's Present Papers and Discuss Them	.47

Note: A value of 1.00 means everyone rated the method favorably while a value of 0.00 means no one rated it favorably.

those [students] that have done well — that is, that have advanced farthest in the traditional school system — are those most in favor of continuing to use methods that have served them well in the past [i.e., lecture]. (p. 208)

Students tended to rate an instructional method highly if it is practical (it allows them to see how they will use what they are learning when they graduate) or if the students have been successful with it in the past. We believe students enjoy practical activities both because these activities provide opportunities to use what they are learning and because these activities allow students to imagine what it will feel like to have completed their studies and have taken jobs in their fields of interest (both of which are issues bearing on identity development).

We believe the more poorly received instructional methods, in contrast, tended to be either not well known to all students (such as computer assisted instruction), perceived by students as 'a lot of work' (such as writing assignments), or offering what might be considered serious threats of embarrassment to students who perform poorly (such as presenting papers in a seminar format).

There was one very interesting exception to the general conclusion about the similarity in response of all groups to the instructional methods, and it involved one of the rarely seen interactions between the Age and College variables. Specifically, the group project's mean is 0.82 for Young Adult Undergraduate with means for the other five groups ranging from 0.47 to 0.65. In other words, Young Adult Undergraduates preferred small group projects more often than would be expected given both how other Young Adults rated the activity and how Adult Undergraduates rated it. We suspect the high rating from younger Undergraduates is explained by the fact that group activities are seen by people in late adolescence as 'fun' because they involve peers and, in doing so, address age appropriate developmental needs.

Group activities are less attractive to students of the same age in the Graduate and Professional colleges because they either have been enculturated into those Colleges and thus see group activities as somehow less appropriate, or they have already passed the developmental point which values group activities highly. Further, the increased time pressure these students experience means they resent the time they have to put in arranging group meetings, coordinating efforts, and handling logistics. These students likely consider that the 'overhead costs' of working in groups are simply not worth the effort. *Steve (A, G)* summed up this view. He said, 'I found that when I took undergraduate classes as part of my graduate work, I was very frustrated working in small groups. Graduate students can set their own level of involvement and don't want to have to rely on others'. We will discuss this issue again when we consider evaluation strategies.

Educational Implications

All in all, students generally prefer instructional approaches showing how they will use the knowledge or skill they are learning. Further, they want to be involved, to have an idea of what it feels like to use what they are learning. Practical projects, individual and group projects, case studies, and discussion of relevant work experience encourage students to apply theory and knowledge to learning activities which give them a vehicle for understanding the material they are learning in a 'real-life' situation. Similarly, simulations give students the opportunity to 'do something' with the knowledge and skills they are studying, applying and testing what they learn in realistic settings. These experiences provide muscle to the skeleton of abstract knowledge and offer exercises allowing those muscles to be strengthened. Thus, for collegiate instruction to be effective, teachers presenting it should help students make the connections between theory and practice not only in their lectures and discussions with students, but in other learning activities as well.

After examining a group of students sharing many characteristics with Graduate participants in our study, Schmidt (1984) advised professors that Graduate students

- prefer to work independently, though under a teacher's direction,
- don't like competitive class activities,
- did not especially want to develop a warm social relationship with the faculty or their peers,

Table 3: Characteristics of best college teachers

Characteristic	Undergraduate	College Graduate	Professional	Total
Organized	.33	.50	.46	.43
Knowledgeable	.30	.46	.33	.37
Communication	.28	.36	.35	.33
Challenging	.28	.32	.30	.30
Cares about Students	.35	.19	.22	.26
Enthusiasm	.14	.25	.25	.21

- saw class as a way of making connections between theory and practice, and
- saw class as a comfortable setting for testing new ideas and challenging view points of peers and teachers.

Again we see the repeated theme of the need for the professor to make a connection between theory and practice for learning.

Best Teachers and Worst Teachers

Best Teacher

We asked respondents to the survey to think of the best college teacher they had had and describe that individual as a teacher and as a person. Specifically, we asked for three characteristics of that instructor's teaching that contributed most to student learning and three of the instructor's personal characteristics that contributed most to student learning.

Using the non-standard-error based techniques described in Appendix A, six teaching attributes of the best college teachers were identified: (i) good organization and preparation, (ii) knowledgeable, (iii) able to communicate, (iv) cared about students, (v) showed enthusiasm for their subject, and (vi) were challenging and demanding. Graphic displays called *stars* (see Chambers *et al.*, 1983; du Toit *et al.*, 1986) were created for each group using these attributes as variables (see Table 3 and Figure 6).

No differences greater than 10 per cent (the minimum difference we considered to be 'educationally important') were found in the stars for Young Adults *versus* Adults, although we did find differences attributable to the three Colleges. First, both Graduate and Professional students reported caring more about the instructor's organizational skills and enthusiasm for the subject than did Undergraduates. This may be because Graduate and Professional students pursue a particular area of study because they care very deeply about it, are in the process of adopting the

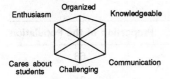

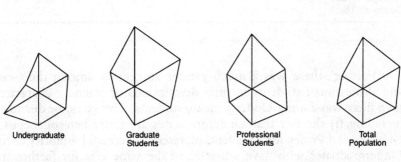

Figure 6: Stars representing the attributes of best teachers for Undergraduates, Graduates, Professional students, and the total population

values of the area they are studying, and consequently appreciate instructors who reflect these feelings and values.

In contrast, Undergraduates were much more concerned than Graduate and Professional students that their professors cared about them — an attribute we would have expected to appear in the description of personal characteristics. *Jimmy (A,U)* described a good teacher by saying, 'Let me describe her [as someone] who is fair, concerned about her students and a very good teacher. If at any time you need help, she is available and she does whatever she can to make the work easier for us'. In other words, while the postgraduate groups looked to instructors to validate the importance of the subject matter, Undergraduate students looked for validation of themselves as persons and/or students. This speculation is consistent with the identity needs of Young Adults, and addresses concerns Adult Undergraduates may have about their abilities to thrive in a college classroom.

It is also consistent with the findings of others. Phoenix (1987), for example, using a methodology based on observation of best and worst teachers rather than reports of students, concluded that best teachers spent much more time accepting students' feelings and praising and using their ideas than did worst teachers. And she cites others (such as Ebel, 1972; McKeachie, 1978) as noting the same things. While she did not consider why it is that teachers who are more accepting of students are rated more highly, we suggest that her data can be explained the same way as ours: Good teachers of Undergraduates validate their students as persons, and they do it by being accepting of the students and their ideas. We will return to this important issue shortly.

Table 4: Personal attributes of best teachers

Attribute	Proportion of the Population
Cares about Students	.68
Open	.40
Sense of Humor	.24
Attitude Toward Work	.22
Desire to Teach	.22

Further, there was a much greater agreement among the Graduate and Professional students in their descriptions of teaching characteristics than there was among Undergraduate students. This could be due to causes including (i) the fact that Undergraduates are more heterogeneous (i.e., Graduate and Professional students represent a successful minority of former Undergraduates who have self-selected the same area for further study); (ii) increased sophistication about what constitutes a 'best teacher'; and (iii) the aging of memories with the passage of time since these people were Undergraduates.

When the students were asked to identify the personal characteristics of their best teacher, the items mentioned most frequently by all categories were: (i) cared about students; (ii) open in perspective; (iii) enjoyed teaching and had a desire to teach; (iv) had a good attitude toward their work; and (v) had a sense of humor or were witty. All Age and College groups of students showed comparable proportions selecting each attribute, and so only pooled proportions are presented in Table 4.

We were intrigued by the fact that 'cares about students' appeared in both the teaching and personal descriptions of best teachers. We noted earlier that Undergraduates raised this issue under the heading of teaching because they look to their teachers to validate them as people, and we wish to qualify that assertion now. Specifically, as students complete their Undergraduate careers and begin Graduate and Professional programs, they come to see themselves less as students and more as members of the professions they have chosen. Simultaneously, they work more closely with the teachers who help them to learn the knowledge, develop the skills, and adopt the belief systems of their professions. In both cases, this means their identities are evolving: They move from requiring reassurances that they have made appropriate career choices to feeling both more secure with their career decisions and more in need of help in becoming professionals. In the Graduate and Professional case, they also come to know their teachers well enough that they can separate faculty as teachers from faculty as people. This means they can see and discuss their teachers both (i) as providers of knowledge about, skill with, and attitudes toward the profession; and (ii) as individuals whom they may or may not like as people.

Table 5: *Teaching characteristics of worst college teachers*

Characteristic	Undergraduate	College Graduate	Professional	Total
Uninteresting	.33	.43	.56	.44
Unclear	.42	.37	.29	.36
Unprepared	.27	.39	.31	.32
Disorganized	.17	.32	.34	.27
Attitude	.24	.23	.25	.24

Worst Teacher

Students were also asked to think of their least effective college teacher and describe that person as a teacher and as a person. Teaching characteristics most often mentioned were (i) uninteresting; (ii) unprepared; (iii) unclear; (iv) bad attitude; and (v) disorganized.

Interestingly, the characteristics of the best and worst teachers were not mirror images of each other; while being challenging and demanding characterizes best teachers, for example, presenting no challenges and making no demands on students are not necessarily the characteristics of a worst teacher. Similarly, knowledgeable is not the opposite of unprepared; *Charles* told us that while he never questioned whether this worst professor knew the material, he did wonder whether the teacher had taken the time to organize his thinking before he entered the classroom.

There were differences among Colleges in what a worst teacher was like. Table 5 and Figure 6 show that Graduate and Professional students are much more likely than Undergraduate students to characterize worst teachers as uninteresting and disorganized. 'The teacher that I like the least was both disinterested in what he was teaching and unprepared for class. I felt that it was a waste of my — and the other students' — time. I just went away with a bad feeling because I felt like my time was wasted', says *Steve (A,G)*. *Robert (A,P)* adds:

> The ineffective ones seem to have forgotten what it was like to learn themselves. The material is taught at a pace that's inappropriate or at a level that's beyond the grasp of the student; ineffective teachers are people who don't organize well; instructors that don't give you cognitive hooks where you can place things in your mind; and professors who test inappropriately.

What constitutes an inappropriate test? Recall that Graduate and Professional students have specific expectations for what they will learn and how they will use their new knowledge and skills. An inappropriate test, then, is one not focused on what they are learning and how they will use it. It matters little whether the lack of focus is due to inappropriate choice

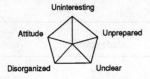

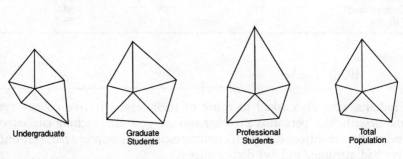

Undergraduate Graduate Students Professional Students Total Population

Figure 7: Stars representing the attributes of worst teachers for Undergraduates, Graduates, Professional students, and the total population

of material covered on the test or the use of questions which are ambiguous or otherwise misleading.

Table 5 and Figure 7 also show that there is generally less agreement among Undergraduates about the characteristics of worst teachers — just as was the case with best teachers. However, Undergraduates were in considerable agreement that being unclear was a common problem among worst teachers. Graduate and Professional students mentioned this less often in describing worst teachers and, we suspect, this is because they long ago mastered alternative ways of learning information; if they are not able to pick it up in class, they can use their own resources to learn it on their own. *Robert (A,P)* describes the situation in medical school: 'Students in medical school tend to learn more or less because they know how to learn. They [sometimes] learn in spite of their professors'. Indeed, a study of medical students' perceptions of teaching indicated that use of away-from-lecture learning increases as the quality of teaching decreases (Slotnick and Durkovic, 1975).

A professor who has a bad attitude toward teaching and students is a much greater concern to the Young Adults than the Adults (Table 6 and Figure 8). *Charles (YA,U)* describes a least liked teacher saying 'He tends to be real spotty and isn't consistent in his lectures. He is very involved in his own research and thinking but isn't involved in his teaching or with people'. We think that the most important part of *Charles'* observation concerns the teacher's lack of involvment with people and his pre-occupation with his own research. Since Young Adults are in the process of separating themselves from their families of origin, they are in particular need of support — in the form of validation of themselves as emerging Adults.

Table 6: *Personal characteristics of worst college teachers*

| | **Age** | | |
Characteristic	*Young Adult*	*Adult*	*Total*
Uninteresting	.39	.49	.44
Unprepared	.32	.32	.32
Unclear	.38	.34	.32
Disorganized	.24	.30	.27
Attitude	.32	.17	.27

Figure 8: Young Adults' and Adults' views of worst teachers

Teachers who do not respond to them as people fail to provide this kind of support, and since Young Adults lack the experience allowing them to separate faculty as teachers from faculty as people, they think poorly of teachers who ignore them.

Adults, in contrast, report uninteresting as more characteristic of worst teachers than do Young Adults. We believe this is because Adults expect faculty to share their interests in the material taught in class, and because an uninteresting teacher tells Adults, in essence, that they have wasted time attending class. This is especially irritating to Adults because they can think of any number of other ways in which they might have better used their time.

We also asked students to list three personal attributes of the worst teacher, attributes that hindered their learning (Table 7 and Figure 9). There was considerable agreement on these characteristics: Dysfunctional teachers tend to be (i) arrogant; (ii) cold; (iii) unenthusiastic; and (iv) unavailable. The Adults identified arrogance more often as a characteristic of a worst teacher than did the Young Adults, and lack of enthusiasm for the

Table 7: Personal characteristics of worst college teachers

| | **College** | | | **Age** | | |
Characteristic	Under-graduate	Graduate	Professional	Young Adult	Adult	Total
Arrogant	.68	.72	.70	.64	.76	.69
Cold	.59	.87	.49	.66	.64	.65
Unenthusiastic	.40	.39	.56	.51	.40	.45
Unavailable	.17	.22	.20	.19	.21	.20

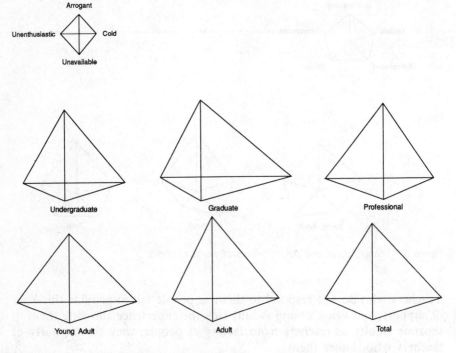

Figure 9: Personal characteristics of worst teachers

subject appears to have a greater impact on Professional students than Graduate students. In the former case, it is possible that Young Adults accept arrogance (do they expect this kind of behavior from some people in positions of authority?) while Adults (who are better able to separate the faculty as teacher from the faculty as a person) are less tolerant of this personality trait. In the latter case, both the law and medical students are making a big financial and time commitment by attending school and are pursuing an area of great interest to them; under these circumstances, an unenthusiastic instructor is abhorrent. Besides, the instructor in medicine and law is more often than not a physician or a lawyer, and thus a potential role model for professional students. This is an important issue because of implications it carries for students' identity development. Conversely, an unenthusiastic instructor flies in the face of the considerable commitment they have made.

Educational Implications

While students are in rough agreement about what constitutes good versus bad teaching, there are nevertheless differences among students attributable to College and Age. Graduate and Professional students, for example, found enthusiasm to be more important than did Undergraduates, while Undergraduates were much more concerned about their instructors' caring about students and enjoying teaching. In other words, Graduate and Professional students want the instructor to validate the subject while Undergraduates want the instructor to validate them.

Undergraduates were also more concerned with lack of clarity than were Graduate and Professional students. Since Undergraduates lack the knowledge and sophistication of their post-baccalaureate counterparts — knowledge and sophistication that comes with completing a bachelor's degree — they need information delivered in a much more precise and direct manner. Age related differences included Young Adults' being concerned about teachers with a bad attitude while Adults resented uninteresting instructors. Since a bad attitude can certainly be personalized and uninteresting has a stronger link with subject matter, we again assert that the Young Adults are displaying greater personal needs, while Adults show greater subject matter oriented needs.

What then, are the instructional implications? We are hard pressed to improve upon the eight suggestions Apps (1981) makes to teachers: Know the biographies of students (thus validating them as persons), use learners' experiences as class content (thus validating subject matter), provide a climate conducive to learning, offering variety in format and technique (so students who do have difficulties with one instructional format can profit from another), provide feedback, help learners acquire resources, and be available to learners for out-of-class contacts. If a teacher does these things, students will find their needs nicely met — whether personal or career needs predominate.

Deterrents

Our study examined students who were already attending college and thus we have no information on people who, for whatever reasons, wanted to enroll but were unable to do so. This means we have no data bearing on deterrents that kept people from participating in educational programs. However, since the literature in this area is rich, a brief discussion of it will describe the challenges facing people wanting to become fulltime adult students. Further, having worked through a problem in the past does not mean the same issue will not re-appear later on; knowing about problems solved in the past provides some information about those that may need to be solved again in the future.

Darkenwald and Merriam (1982) found that personal problems were the greatest deterrent to participation in educational programs. Those suggesting this as a major deterrent were most often female (81 per cent), and indicated problems with child care and competing family responsibilities and, to lesser extents, health problems, handicaps, and uneasiness about the location of the courses.

The second major deterrent was lack of self-confidence. It is not difficult to imagine adults in pre-admission counseling sessions saying,

'I'm too old to learn'.
'I can't compete with those kids'.
'I've been out of school twenty years; I'll never make it'.
'I'm afraid of making a fool out of myself'.
and 'I'm not smart enough'.

Though these concerns dissipate with the experience of being in school, they are very important to adults who are considering returning to school. Indeed, they may not have dissipated for the people who didn't attend.

Two other factors mentioned were (i) lack of personal interest in participation in organized education, and (ii) an interest in education but a lack of programs relevant to their needs and interests.

Surprisingly, cost was mentioned infrequently; it was lowest on the list of concerns. Respondents identifying this as a deterrent were most often female and, on average, were younger than the other adults in the sample.

In looking at health professionals specifically, Scanlan and Darkenwald (1984) identified six factors keeping people from returning to school. They included disengagement — uncertainty, boredom, apathy, etc.; dissatisfaction with the quality of programs available; family constraints — time away from family; cost; weight of costs vs. the value of the benefits; and work constraints — scheduling difficulties, conflicting demands.

We assume that Adult students enrolling in higher education have considered both the costs and benefits of returning to school, and that the cost-benefit ratio favors enrolling. The fact that they have determined that school is relevant to their needs does not mean that all the forces working against their decision have been resolved. We shall see that issues of time, money, and balancing the different demands in their lives continue to be a challenge to the Adult student.

Obstacles

All adults who wish to enroll face problems we have already described: family, finances, jobs, and the like. When these problems keep a person from enrolling, we refer to them as deterrents; when students are able to overcome them, we call them obstacles. In other words, the issues described in the following pages are problems encountered and handled by students enrolled at our University.

Even (1987) suggests a metaphor for obstacles, and that is 'baggage'. Each adult comes with baggage: sometimes the baggage is heavy and is made up of money problems, family problems, and job problems; for others, the baggage is lighter and allows students the freedom of time, good self-esteem, a lighter heart, and a stronger spirit. In her book *Adults as Learners*, K. Patricia Cross (1981) classifies the obstacles to education students face as situational, institutional, and dispositional. *Situational barriers* are those arising from one's real life situation: money and time are scarce; home and job responsibilities interfere; needs for child care and transportation have to be met; there is no good place to study; and frequently friends and family are opposed to the student's educational pursuits. *Institutional barriers* arise from typical administrative, organizational, and educational practices: restrictive class schedules make it difficult to pursue a coherent course of study; procedural red tape means spending valuable hours and energy in registration, financial matters, and program planning; and entry requirements are often inappropriate for older persons. *Dispositional barriers* are those related to attitudes and self-perceptions about oneself as a learner.

Because we were unsure of differences among students in terms of the obstacles they had to face, we asked respondents to describe the most difficult obstacle they had overcome in their current university studies. Although the scree test results showed little agreement among the students of different age and college, we were nevertheless able to make several observations.

First, the obstacles students faced fell nicely into Cross' three categories (see Table 8 and Figure 10). The biggest situational barrier among Professional students was concern about money. Law and medical students cannot work fulltime, are not eligible for graduate assistantships, and class and study demands preclude all but minimal parttime work.

Time to balance home, work, and family also appear to be a greater concern for Adult than Young Adult students. This is consistent with a national study conducted for the Commission on Non-Traditional Study (Carp, Peters, and Roelfs, 1974), which found that adult learners felt cost, not enough time, and home responsibilities were the greatest barriers to their educations.

We recall *Jerry's (A,P)* comments about time: 'If I could sum up the barriers in one word, it is time. You simply don't have enough time to do

Table 8: *Obstacles faced by students*

	College			Age		
Obstacle	Under-graduate	Graduate	Professional	Young Adult	Adult	Total
Money	.11	.11	.11	.13	.24	.19
Balancing Demands	.20	.22	.09	.11	.24	.18
Bureaucracy	.13	.12	.04	.15	.09	.12
Studying	.13	.09	.10	.08	.13	.11
Time	.05	.13	.11	.05	.10	.08

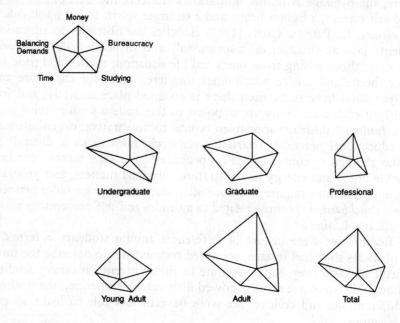

Figure 10: *Obstacles faced by students*

everything'. *Jerry* also feels Young Adults are not bothered by time demands. 'If you are a traditional aged student', he observes, 'there just aren't the kind of pressures that we older-than-average students face'.

Amber (A,P) reflected on institutional barriers which irritate the Adult learner.

> If you have worked out in the business world, it is extremely difficult to have to deal with a system that requires you to walk all the way across campus to pick up a paper, take it back somewhere else and get it signed, then walk all the way across

Table 9: *Self-ratings of skills by students from different colleges*

| | **Type of College** | |
Type of Skill	Undergraduate	Graduate and Professional
Scientific Research	.40	.60
Study Skills	.63	.80
Writing Skills	.76	.87

Note: A value of 1.00 meant everyone felt they were strong in the area indicated; a value of 0.00 meant no one felt they were strong.

campus to turn the paper in but not be able to do anything with it on that occasion, then have to go all the way back across campus and come back at another occasion and sit around for several hours twiddling your thumbs to get in to see somebody. Making appointments is extremely difficult with the University system. I don't have time to spare. I need to be able to call and set up a time and expect that person to be there. And that person can expect that I will be there and we can transact our business and then we will be done. This [inefficient time utilization] is not responsive to the demands on the time of any student but particularly the older-than-average student.

In short, Adults faced the variety of obstacles Cross described, and they faced them successfully. Solutions to the problem did not come easily, however, because Adults needed to allocate scarce resources such as time in solving them. However, the solutions did profit from Adults both having well-developed problem solving skills (coming from their rich experiences) and an understanding of 'the system'.

Personal Academic Strengths and Weaknesses

Our study showed that College — and not Age — provided the differences in perceived strengths and weaknesses: Graduate and Professional students perceived themselves as having better writing, computer, and study skills than did Undergraduates (see Table 9). This is understandable since to be admitted to either of these programs, students must have demonstrated well-developed scholarly skills. In other words, Graduate and Professional students are a self-selected, demonstrably successful population — arguably, and as a group, the most scholarly of the former Undergraduates.

Jerry (A,P) says, 'In order to get into Graduate and Professional [school], you have to demonstrate the ability to write cohesively and analytically', while *Britt (YA,P)* observes, 'As an Undergraduate, you're not challenged to write. As a Graduate or Professional student you're expected to be a better writer'. An Undergraduate student indicated that the experience with writing in Graduate and Professional schools gives students more practice, and thus improved abilities and self-confidence.

Graduate and Professional students also rated themselves higher than Undergraduates in study skills. Our interviews indicate that growing self-discipline, commitment, ability to balance competing commitments, a sense of purpose, and knowledge of program expectations contribute to better study skills. *Amber (A,P)* reflects,

> Graduate and Professional students *must* have better study skills because of the burden of time and energy. For the most part, Graduate and Professional students are balancing more things; they are trying to juggle home, family, jobs and school. So, like the old adage, you don't work harder, you work smarter. You become more efficient at what you have to do.

Britt (YA,P) says, 'You have more purpose as a Graduate or Professional student. You are building a foundation for something that will be your career forever'. *Jerry (A,P)* agrees: 'It's the environment here. You're making a commitment to Professional and Graduate [school] and unless you apply yourself, you are using up some of the most productive years of your life. School is a big financial commitment, too'. It is true that people likely to be accepted into Graduate and Professional programs are those who have already demonstrated their abilities in academic areas; their study skills, for example, may always have been better than those of the other Undergraduates who either do not apply for Adult education or are not accepted. Further, the fact that they have worked in areas of interest to them is inherently motivating; it is another reason to find ways to study harder and study better.

Graduate and Professional students also rated themselves higher in scientific research skills than did Undergraduates. *Jimmy (A,U)* believes that Graduate and Professional students have more experience and opportunities to work with active research teams (whether in the laboratory, the field, or the library), and therefore they develop stronger skills.

Other students we interviewed concurred with *Jimmy's* analysis. *Charles (YA,U)* says, 'Graduate and Professional students have the experience [in scientific research]. Typical Undergraduates are just not going to have the chance to develop that [skill]'. Similarly, *Britt (YA,P)* reflects, 'Graduate programs require a lot of research. Simply by having to do it you acquire more skill'. 'It's required of you as a Graduate and Professional student and that makes you better at it', observes *Billie Jo (YA,U)*.

Significant differences were found in the perceptions of skills of Graduate versus Professional students. Self-ratings of computer skills by Graduate students were higher than corresponding self-ratings of Pro-

Table 10:   Campus-wide perceptions of skills

Skill Area	Proportion
Comprehending Instruction	.94
General Problem Solving Skills	.92
Completing Assignments	.90
Reading Skill	.85
Writing Skill	.81
Oral Communication Skill	.78
Computer Skill	.73
Math Skill	.64
Study Skill	.54
Scientific Research	.53

fessional students. *Britt (YA,P)* explains, 'I compare myself to a good friend who's a psychology graduate student. She is on the computer several hours a day, recording and analyzing her data, and medical students really have no use for a computer unless it is simply to look up articles'. *Jerry (A,P)* adds, 'Graduate students may use computers for scientific research. Law students just use them for word processing'. Graduate students, of course, also use computers for literature searching and word processing as well.

Though not shown in Table 9, Young Adult students perceive their math skills to be stronger than Adult students perceive theirs. *Billie Jo (YA,U)* suggests this is because 'The traditional-aged students have math fresh in their minds coming out of high school. If you don't use it, you lose it'. *Jimmy (A,U)* agrees, noting, 'Younger students are still actively in school using their math skills on a constant basis whereas the individuals out in the field may not be using their math skills as often and probably become a bit rusty'. Several other students interviewed pointed out that math assumes less importance as a person grows older unless that person is employed in a scientific field. All reflected that they use math for day-to-day living such as balancing a checkbook, whereas other, more complex, skills are lost because they are not used.

However, we find this difference in math skills ambiguous since others (e.g., Knox, 1976) have observed that Adults attend more closely to accuracy than speed. Thus, if ability is assessed in terms of speed (i.e., how long it takes to complete a problem set), Adults may seem disadvantaged; if ability is measured in the proportion of correct answers, it is less likely that differences will be observed.

Table 10 displays the campus-wide self-assessments of the skills covered in the survey (assessments for all students regardless of Age or College — see Appendix A for details on how these values were computed). The rank ordering of students' assessments of their skills reflects general applicability: The more generally useful the skill, the higher it is rated; alternatively, the skills most useful to only self-selected groups appear

Table 11: *Preference for evaluation strategies by colleges*

	College	
Evaluation Strategies	Graduate and Undergraduate	Professional
Group Projects	.40	.20
Research and Papers	.40	.62
Grading on a Curve	.70	.51

Note: A score of 1.00 indicates everyone preferred the strategy while 0.00 means no one preferred it.

lower on the list. The exception to this generalization is study skills — a general skill appearing near the bottom of the list. Apparently students are not as sanguine about their abilities to study as they are about other skills.

These self-ratings have instructional implications only if there are discrepancies between the abilities of the students and the demands of various curricula. Backus (1984) notes that Adults, on returning to college after a number of years away, are often concerned about their abilities to write, do research, and complete assignments. Often, though, these concerns dissipate as Adults gain experience as students, and so faculty need to consider whether Adults' concerns are due to 're-entry jitters' or more persistent problems.

Since one would expect Graduate and Professional students to have better scholarly tools than the Undergraduate population, scholarly tools is not an issue of concern unless a student with inadequate skills seeks admission to Graduate or Professional programs.

The reported lack of some skills — such as math skills in the Adult group — may be problematic, however. The fact that the Adult student may well have been away from formal education for an extended period of time may account for the loss of some math skills, but that is not important. What is important is that Adult learners may need some remedial assistance in order to 'brush-up' on their skills, or perhaps a class to introduce them to recent developments in math and other related fields. This agrees with Hughes (1983) who found that Adults needed more remedial work, particularly in the area of mathematics.

Preferred Evaluation Strategy

Students in the survey reviewed a list of evaluation strategies and identified those they liked and those they disliked. Significant differences were noted in several areas and are displayed in Table 11.

Graduate and Professional students showed a significantly greater preference for evaluation based on research and papers than did Undergraduates, and students we interviewed hypothesized this was because

Graduate and Professional students enjoy exploring their own areas of interest in depth while Undergraduates see such activities as potentially threatening. *Jimmy (A,U)* says, 'A Graduate or Professional [student] has been out there, he's been applying the principles he has learned, he's gotten confidence in his work, and he feels that on his papers or projects he should be graded accordingly'. *Robert (A,P)* adds:

> When you, as a Graduate or Professional student, write and do research, you are utilizing critical thinking, you're using your own creativity, and you're showing what you know. Undergraduate students, I suspect, haven't become comfortable with those skills yet. They don't know how to show what they know and so probably feel more comfortable just being asked questions. The funny thing is that medical students tend to be the same way.

(This latter point is evidence that, on the continuum from Undergraduate to Graduate, Professional students fall somewhere in the middle.)

Undergraduate students showed a greater preference for being evaluated on group projects than did Graduate and Professional students. Students interviewed agreed that Undergraduates, regardless of age, show greater preference for group projects because of the support, security, social interaction, and camaraderie of group work. Some also saw it as an easy way out and the employment of the 'safety in numbers' theory, as explained by *Daniel (YA,G)* who believes, 'As an undergraduate, you'd rather work with a group so that if you don't know something, hopefully somebody else does and as a team you can solve the problem'. *Naomi (A,U)* reports, 'Undergraduates like the support they get from a group, whereas older or more advanced students feel that this is a waste of their time'. *Amber (A,P)* laughingly adds, 'I'll bet those Undergraduates haven't had that much experience with a group project where only one person did the work and that person happened to be you'.

Adult students showed a significantly greater preference for evaluation based on research and papers than Young Adult students (Table 12). *Britt (YA,P)* believes that:

> Older people have more experience to draw from and I think that is so valuable. When you're young, it's hard to write a paper if you don't know anything and you can't contribute any prior knowledge. In our class, I find this is really something I lack. Our older students just seem more able to think of things in a wider scope and use their past experiences. An older student in our class has this really broad view of things; he can see the whole picture. As a younger student, you'd rather just have something to answer and not write or expound on it.

Table 12: *Preference for evaluation strategies by age*

	Age Group	
Evaluation Strategy	Young Adult	Adult
Research Papers	.61	.77
Grading on a Curve	.66	.50

Naomi (A,U) believes that the Adult student's 'quest for knowledge leads to research', while *Jerry (A,P)* suggests that 'research and papers give the [Adult] student an opportunity to demonstrate your knowledge in an area whereas a traditional exam can hit you on a bad day and wouldn't be a fair assessment of what you know'. *Robert (A,P)* says that 'The older student has more experiences that suggest that things are more complex and have more variables. You look to research as a chance to incorporate and broaden your experience. Younger students tend to have more tunnel vision'.

Adult students have more experience and a wider view that allows them to deal better with ambiguity. Young Adults find ambiguity unsettling, and so they like the structure provided by a test.

Apps (1981) found that adult learners want to offer many alternative responses based on life experience, not a simple response recalled from a lecture. Similarly, Hughes (1983) concluded from his study that adult students preferred faculty who based the final grade on several activities, who provided alternative assignments and retests, and who modified course outlines to satisfy student interests.

It is also true that adults exhibit more ease in concept formation than do younger students. As age increases, so does movement from concrete to abstract and the ability to differentiate between concepts, an aspect of cognitive development described earlier in this book. *Steve (A,G)* believes that:

> [Adult students] accept less structure. Just having tests is quite structured. You're studying for this test at this time and you study these chapters whereas writing a paper forces you to organize your thoughts, make decisions, and organize your own time. Younger students want a more structured environment. The older student would rather set his own direction and time frame.

Thus, Adult students would be more comfortable with the critical thinking and the concept formation required to write papers and do research. *Steve (A,G)* adds, 'Adult students have an idea of where they want to go and they can direct themselves', a view congruent with Malcolm Knowles' (1970) suggestion that programs for adults must make heavy use of self-directed learning.

Professional students showed a significantly greater preference for evaluation by examination only than did Graduate students (see Table 13).

Table 13: *Preference for evaluation strategies for Graduate and Professional students*

	College	
Evaluation Strategy	Graduate	Professional
Group Projects	.28	.13
Tests Only	.52	.79

Both medical and law students indicate that, as *Amber (A,P)* says, 'We don't have any choice and we don't know any other way'. Evaluation by examination is the way it is done in the schools of law and medicine.

Although neither Graduate nor Professional students listed evaluation by group projects highly, Graduate students did show a significantly greater preference for this method than did Professional students (see Table 13). Almost all those interviewed agreed that there is more competitiveness in professional schools than in graduate schools, and Professional students view themselves as needing to 'go it alone'. *Britt (YA,P)* says, 'Perhaps Professional students want to be individually rewarded for their performance'. *Amber (A,P)* believes,

> Physicians and attorneys reach that point — when it comes to the courtroom or when you make a diagnosis of the patient — that there's nobody else, you do it by yourself! That gets built into the schooling. It goes back to the self-selection idea of who gets into Professional schools. It's people with strong egos.

When students were asked about grading on a percentage basis (i.e., criteria in terms of the minimum percentage that must be earned to receive a given grade), Professional and Graduate students showed a significantly greater preference than Undergraduates. *Daniel (YA,G)* explains this by saying, 'Everyone does well in graduate school so you don't need a curve. In grad school, you're not really in competition with other students'. *Rhonda (YA,G)* believes that Graduate and Professional students prefer it because 'it's a more absolute scale. You are grading yourself against a set standard instead of whoever happens to be in your class'. *Britt (YA,P)* says, 'In med school, if you get 75 per cent you pass and you've successfully acquired what you need to know for that amount of material. Whereas if we put it on a curve, even if you did fairly well, you'd be at the bottom'.

Young Adult students showed a significantly greater preference for grading on a curve than Adult students. *Daniel (YA,G)* believes:

> Traditional age students rely on the curve. After the first test where you got a 70 and you thought you were getting a C and many others got 70s or below the professor curved it up and you got a B or possibly an A. That's one of the first questions you ask every

semester, 'Do you grade on a curve?' It's a crutch, something you can fall back on if you do poorly. If you're average in class you know you're going to end up all right even though you might have done poorly.

Perhaps this is the 'safety in numbers' idea referred to earlier; if it is, the preference of Young Adults for it may reflect the stage of their identity development.

Adults, on the other hand, preferred to be evaluated through use of criterion-referenced measures (i.e., they wanted to be evaluated in relation to pre-existing standards), while the Young Adults preferred a norm-referenced measure (i.e., they wanted to be evaluated in relation to others). In other words, Young Adults seem to stress the importance of their relationships to their peers ('We'll all sink or swim together'), as opposed to the Adult's desire to address individual needs. The Adult learners preferred to be evaluated individually through such means as papers and individual projects while the Young Adults preferred group projects as an evaluative tool.

There are educational implications here. Young Adults will find the instructor's assessment more meaningful when the evaluation gives them information not only about how well they did on the task, but also how well they are doing in relation to their peers although they will need to be moved in the direction of evaluating themselves on the basis of how they perform. Adults, on the other hand, favor feedback that assesses their skill and growth as individuals and provides them with *a priori* standards useful in this respect.

Support Services

Finally, the students identified the support services that either helped or hindered them during their enrollment at the University. Significant differences appeared in several areas (see Table 13). Undergraduates rated registration and tutoring services significantly higher than did Graduate and Professional students, perhaps because registration is more of an 'occasion' for Undergraduates (it has a social aspect to it), and Undergraduates are more likely than other students to use tutorial services and therefore rate them higher than did the other groups.

Perceptions of support from other students, family, and instructors and advisors revealed several significant differences. Young Adults perceived significantly less support from family than did Adults. We hypothesize that Young Adults were thinking of family as their mothers and fathers whereas Adult students were reflecting on their spouses and children and, once again, this relates to the students' stages in identity development.

Graduate and Professional students perceived greater support from their instructors and advisors ('faculty' in Table 14) since students there

Table 14:   *Ratings of support services by college*

	College	
Support Service	Undergraduate	Graduate and Professional
Registration	2.38	2.14
Tutoring	2.10	1.98
Library	2.55	2.72
Support from Family	2.61	2.77
Support from Faculty	2.44	2.67

Note: A score of 3 indicates students responded positively, a score of 1 indicates a negative response, and a score of 2 neutral.

Table 15:   *Rating of support for Graduate and Professional students*

	College	
Support Service	Graduate	Professional
Parking	1.74	1.59
Computer Facilities	2.48	2.25
Housing	2.21	

Note: A score of 3 indicates students responded positively, a score of 1 indicates a negative response, and a score of 2 neutral.

generally work much more closely with their instructors and advisors (individually and in small classes or small group settings) and so this finding is not surprising.

While all students rated library services as highly supportive, Undergraduate students rated it significantly lower than Graduate and Professional students. Since Graduate and Professional students are both more likely to be familiar with the library and may be required to use library services more in their programs, the finding is also not surprising.

Table 15 shows a significant difference in perception of support services between Graduate and Professional students. Graduate students rated computer facilities significantly higher than Professional students. This is consistent with a finding in another section of this study which shows Graduate students have an appreciably greater comfort with computer skills than Professional students. During the interviews, students hypothesized that this finding reflects the much greater reliance on the use of computers in Graduate school than in Professional school.

All groups rated parking poorly, though Graduate students were less critical of it than were Professional students. We believe this is because many Graduate students have assistantships and therefore can purchase permits to use faculty parking. Further, many graduate classes are offered in the evening when anyone can park in any lot on campus. Professional students, in contrast, must take their classes during the day and compete with Undergraduates for parking spaces in the more remote student lots.

Table 16: *Campus-wide assessments of support and support services*

Source of Support	Mean
Financial Aid Support	2.82
Library Services	2.80
Support from Family	2.62
Support from Students	2.62
Support from Faculty	2.40
Registration Services	2.38
Computer Facilities	2.34
Housing	2.12
Orientation Services	2.10
Placement Services	2.07
Counseling Services	2.04
Tutoring Services	2.03
Child Care Services	1.89
Parking Services	1.49

Note: A score of 3 indicates students responded positively, a score of 1 indicates a negative response, and a score of 2 is neutral.

The campus-wide perceptions of support and support services are displayed in Table 16. The same pattern of greatest satisfaction with most commonly used services is seen here and, once again, there is a single exception. Parking is reported to be the least favorable of all the services on campus even though it is used almost universally.

Summary

The two identifiable attributes of students we studied were related to systematic differences among students; Age (Young Adult and Adult) which reflects differences in stage in identity and cognitive development, and College (Undergraduate, Graduate, and Professional). If a faculty member understands, for example, that Young Adult students are still in the process of separating themselves from their families of origin and so they rely heavily on members of their peer groups for a sense of identity, instructional activities can be identified and designed incorporating instruction into formats that simultaneously address this psychological need and the instructional goals of the course. Further, and possibly because these students lack close, regular contact with their teachers, they do not separate teachers as teachers from teachers as persons. A good teacher is, by their view, someone whom they can like, someone who they see as recognizing them as valuable people.

Similarly, instruction in Adult classes should allow the students to be recognized as independent adults who are dealing with a number of competing demands including family, school, and employment.

If the course is at the Undergraduate level, these needs can be addressed by ensuring that students are 'validated' as persons. The teacher who genuinely cares about students will not only be well received by them but will find they learn more than from a teacher they perceive as not caring. Similarly, Graduate and Professional students will learn most when they feel the teacher 'validates' the importance and interest inherent in the material being taught.

Implications for Teaching: Some Suggestions

Deterrents

Although the other educational implications in this book relate to students already in college and generally make recommendations to the faculty, this section will discuss ways to remove some of the barriers to Adult student entry into college and generally make recommendations to administrators.

Since self-confidence seemed to be a major deterrent, particularly for Adult students who feel 'it's been too long, I couldn't compete', or 'I'd be lost in the sea of young faces', students could meet with other students who have 'made it' to answer their questions and allay their fears (they might also want to see the Michael Caine movie entitled *Educating Rita*). Representatives from financial aid also might be present to discuss financial options for Adult students. Put simply, the more questions answered before the student comes onto campus, the less anxiety there is for the potential Adult student.

Many potential Adult students feel that their math and writing skills are too rusty to provide them an adequate base for a successful college experience. If Universities and Colleges are interested in attracting this pool of students, the schools need to provide non-credit 'refresher' courses that are inexpensive for students. The courses would help students brush up these important skills prior to entry into college. They are also described in greater detail in the next chapter.

Support Services

While support services such as registration, tutoring, parking and library will probably not, in and of themselves, determine whether or not students will be successful in college, these services can be a major detractor from the college experience, especially for the Adult student with limited time. College administrators will be well advised to do all they can to reduce barriers for Adult students through the use of telephone registration, extended hours for the library, and tutoring services accessible for the time pressed students.

Since Adult students mentioned family support as being very important to their success, administrators should think of ways to inform and include family members in campus activities. Particularly for the Adult student, family housing would have more importance than dorm parties. Indeed, special attention should be paid to family housing, since this will be important to the Adult.

Chapter 6

Recommendations for Teaching Adult Students

Gilda Radner on Being an Adult Learner

A member of our research team commented on the experience of being an Adult Learner.

> Being an Adult Learner is different. You have the same things to do in class as Young Adults, sure. But outside of class there are so many other things you have to do. It's like Gilda Radner used to say, 'It's always something'. And you sure do appreciate teachers who understand that.

Introduction

We make recommendations in this chapter for working with Adult students. While we do not concern ourselves specifically with Young Adults, many of the suggestions we make apply to them as well; as described in the introduction to Part II, the absence of statistical interactions means that comments about Undergraduates, for example, bear on all Undergraduates regardless of age (and the same is true for Graduate and Professional students). Our focus, though, is on Adults.

Recommendations on teaching Adults are appropriate both because there are important differences between Young Adult and Adult Learners and because the number of Adult learners on campus is considerable and continues to grow. Adults differ from Young Adults both in terms of their expectations for what education will be like, and the other demands made on their time. These differences need to be considered by skillful teachers — teachers who understand that students are multidimensional, multifaceted people.

Unfortunately, not all college teachers believe Adult and Young Adult students differ. Some faculty still entertain a misconception, possibly due to the lack of important differences between these two groups in terms of their preferences for different instructional strategies. These faculty seem to think that, since both populations feel the same way about instructional strategies, they must be alike in all other regards. Our research confirms that the two groups are similar in their preferences for instructional strategies, but our findings underscore the fact that there are other important ways in which Adult and Young Adult students differ, ways bearing on how and how much students in each group can learn.

These differences include the reasons for being in school (Chapter 4), expectations students have for what will occur there (Chapter 3), the students' developmental status (Chapter 2), demands on students' resources (such as time and money as described in Chapter 4), and their obligations (to family and job, as presented in Chapter 1). In other words, while there are similarities between Young Adult and Adult students concerning preferences for instructional strategies, a more holistic perspective shows the two groups to be very different in very important ways.

This chapter explores the ramifications of these differences for faculty and universities, and it does so following a particular format. Each section begins with information reviewing our findings (and those of others, as appropriate) as a prelude to the recommendations. Each section ends with specific suggestions useful in implementing the recommendations.

Recommendations for Faculty

Background

There are things faculty and universities can do to facilitate the learning of Adult students, actions which can be justified through the research described in the preceding chapters. We begin with recommendations for faculty.

Recommendation for Instructional Strategies

Though there are no important differences between Adults' and Young Adults' preferences for instructional strategies, students (regardless of age) do prefer certain instructional techniques over others. In some cases, preference is a matter of each individual's personal learning style, while in other cases, it reflects the fact that some colleges use specific strategies more than others (the Schools of Law and Medicine, for example, rely heavily on lectures, and so lectures appear especially popular with legal and medical students).

Of the thirteen instructional methods we considered, three were clearly more popular than the others (see Table 2): practical projects, lectures with discussion, and use of simulations. The feature shared by these three is that all actively involve the student. To help students become and remain active, we propose:

Recommendation 1:   *Faculty should demonstrate the range of ways in which students will use what they're learning (students should be able to say, 'This is how I'll apply what we're learning').*

Implicit in this recommendation is the precept well known to good teachers: Good teachers know their students. This means learning not only their names, but also knowing about their backgrounds and goals for the course they're taking. This latter point includes both the things they expect of instruction, and the ways in which they will use what they learn in their personal and professional lives. In describing Adult learners, Knox (1986) says this means first appreciating their attributes and then moving to specific students' characteristics:

> Paradoxically, generalizations about adults as learners are useful not so much to guide your teaching as to guide your understanding of the individual participants in each program. Effective teaching depends on being responsive to the learners in the program, not to adults in general. (p. 38)

Thus, teaching such things as a new concept or skill means helping students understand its applicability to them (a point also made by Knox [1989]), and this task can be approached in a variety of ways. Examples (whether contrived or based on real events) can be used, but they must be presented in sufficient detail so the practical applications of the ideas are clear. Another approach is to describe the way class members will use the new concepts and principles in their careers. For example, in a statistics class taught as part of an MBA program, the teacher might say, 'Kelly, pretend you're running a plant manufacturing electric motors. Here's how you can use measures of central tendency to reduce the number of faulty motors your plant produces'. In doing this, the instructor both shows the applicability of what she is teaching and allows students (both Kelly and the others in class) to see how they'll use it after they graduate.

The more immediate the applicability, the more likely students will value what they are learning. This means the judicious teacher will select examples from the students' current experiences rather than fabricate more remote, less believable scenarios. The electric motors example would be most valuable if Kelly were already working in an electric motor plant.

Interestingly, immediacy depends on whether the Adults are in school to take on a first or new career versus advancing in their current career. The reason for this is that persons preparing to enter a career have notions about what they will do which are different from those of practicing professionals. Beginning medical students, for example, have little appreciation of the importance of communication skills or being a self-guided learner to practicing physicians.

The implication of this point is that, for these students, examples must be relevant *given what they understand the practice of the career they seek to be like.* This may be a very different example than is appropriate for persons in school to advance their careers, people who already have an accurate perspective of what they will be doing when they finish their studies.

Regardless of students' expectations for how they'll use what's taught, allowing students to imagine themselves in professional roles is a good teaching tactic. Using imagery is good because, while it makes the application of the material taught more 'real', its primary value is in allowing students to see themselves actively applying what they are learning. This is an important aspect of instruction because it contributes to identity development. In this way, the use of examples involving students leads directly to our next suggestion:

Recommendation 2: *Faculty should actively involve students in their own learning.*

Some researchers (such as Knox, 1986) discuss this as a requirement for instruction generally while others are more specific noting that passivity is the single biggest weakness in lecturing. This last point is important because lecturing is arguably the most commonly used instructional format in universities, and so we will return to the issue of making students active in lectures shortly.

Helping students to be active in projects and classroom activities is not difficult. When students pick the project they are to work on, they feel invested in it, and they are invested in simulations because their realistic nature allows students to see how the things they are learning apply in the real world. In short, realistic simulations contribute both to students' knowledge and the development of their professional identities.

Student participation can also be encouraged in ways that are less time-consuming than projects and full-blown simulations. For example, when the class considers an important principle, students can be provided with a list of problems and asked to choose the one(s) they would like considered in class. This is effective because it allows students the opportunity to consider the similarities and differences inherent in the range of circumstances where the principle applies and it gives them a degree of control over the class' functioning while the teacher retains ultimate control because she provided the list of problems to choose from. The teacher must nevertheless retain the right to make sure that certain problems are covered so that all major applications of the principle are covered. She would exercise this option, for example, if the class did not consider any examples of a particular class of problem.

It is a short step from problems selected by students to problems proposed by students. Here, it is a virtual certainty that some students' interests will be addressed, and that is important. It is important because, given that the students in the class share common interests (which is why they are enrolled in the same class), it is also likely that a notable fraction of the students will appreciate any problem nominated for discussion.

Student activity can also be fostered in lectures. Indeed, student passivity is the single biggest problem with lectures (e.g., McKeachie, 1978; and McLeish, 1976). A straightforward way to approach this problem is through questioning, and effective questioning requires calling on students by name. Names can be managed simply by using tent cards (5″ × 8″ cards folded lengthwise) on which students write their names with a wide-tipped marker and then place on their desks. When desks are arranged in rows and columns, the teacher can then read the cards from the front of the room and so address each student by name; if the seats are arranged in a U-shape or circle, everyone can know everyone else's name — a real advantage when students do not know each other. Helping students to get acquainted is part of providing a supportive learning environment [Knox, 1986]). (It is crucial that teachers bring the tent cards to class everyday and collect them at class' end; they will be forgotten by the students otherwise.)

Other simple procedures include a seating chart. After students have decided which seats they'll use, have them 'sign up' for them.

Another suggestion involves what to do when the student doesn't know the answer. Students know if they only sit quietly (usually looking down at their notebooks), after a while the teacher will either re-address the question to someone else or answer it herself. In return for a few moments of discomfort, the student has avoided the responsibility of not having the answer for a question.

An alternative way to handle this situation is to say to the student, 'Chris, do you need some help?' and, when the student says 'Yes', the teacher responds by saying, 'OK. Ask someone in the class to help you'. The student, initially with a little encouragement from the teacher, will then call on another student for help in answering the question.

This technique has much to commend it. It lets students know it's all right not to know an answer — which preserves the dignity of the student who does not know the answer (this is especially important for Adults who are taking their first courses and are concerned about being able to succeed in the classroom). It also starts discussions in the classroom because two students are now working at answering the question.

Another easily implemented and effective technique is the 'programmed' lecture (Manning, 1965). At the beginning of the lecture, the teacher distributes a list of questions, questions students reasonably can be expected to know. Instructions on the sheet tell students not to answer any of the questions until told to do so, and, at the point when the topic associated with the first question is to be considered, students are instructed to answer the question — in writing — in the space provided on the sheet. After waiting long enough for almost all students to complete the question, the lecturer asks for answers and writes them *verbatim* on the blackboard. Once a number of answers have been transcribed in this way, the lecture continues as a discussion considering the nominated answers. The lecturer, of course, maintains the responsibility for making sure all important points are covered regardless of whether they are nominated by the students.

The activity engages students actively by having them write out their answers, and it also attracts and maintains their attention in other ways. Each student wants to know, for example, if they 'got the right answer' for the question, and they pay careful attention in the process of finding out.

Repetition of the question, transcription of answers, and a lecture/discussion cycle keep an otherwise large lecture (such as one presented to several hundred students) from becoming boring. It breaks up the lecturer's talking with inherently motivating activity on the parts of the students.

It is critical to remember that differences in preference for instructional formats can be attributed to both college and individual preference though not age. This means that when a student has difficulty learning something, it is well to consider whether the manner of preparation of material is appropriate to that student's needs. A common problem is one in which a holistic learner (who needs an initial overview of what is being taught) is treated as if she were an analytic learner (who learns by relating things learned to one another). Skillful teachers, in working with students who are having difficulties with learning, consider how the student's learning style 'fits' the way instruction is conducted.

Three of the five instructional strategies in the second cluster (see Table 2) involved small group activities: study groups, seminars, and group projects. Though we have evidence that Adult learners have concerns about the use of group learning activities, the fact is that they are widely used because they address important educational goals such as teaching problem solving and developing interpersonal skills. Because they are heavily used, we offer a recommendation concerning their use with Adults:

Recommendation 3: *Faculty must be certain Adults' needs are addressed when they work at group activities.*

This recommendation addresses the fact that many Adults are uncomfortable with group learning activities, and this discomfort grows from several sources. First, Adults' developmental needs do not involve groups (they see themselves as individuals and not group members); second, Adults' time constraints imply that scheduling group activities will be difficult, and third, Adults have a marked intolerance of group members not appearing to be doing their share.

The latter problem is very much the teacher's responsibility; teachers need to make sure students in each group know what they are to do and are evaluated according to whether they do it. Without this, Adult students stand both to learn less than they might from small group activities and to see group activities as non-productive. They also become very unsatisfied with the instruction they receive.

There is a second implication deriving from Recommendation 3, and it means ensuring that Adult Learners understand that groups have natural histories. Over the history of a group, energy is divided between both group process and task resolution with the amount of energy devoted to each aspect varying according to where the group is in its evolution. Early in the group's development, for example, much more energy is devoted to group process than to working on the group's task, and so it is possible for group members — especially Adults because they are particularly concerned about things like efficient use of their time — to be dissatisfied. This means the skillful teacher will learn about the ways groups develop (see Tuckman, 1965; Tuckman and Jensen, 1977, for example) and will pass that information on to students who can then better understand what is happening in their working groups.

Recommendation Based on Characteristics of Best Teachers

Our study identified a series of characteristics of good teachers, characteristics also identified by other writers. Based on both our findings and the other sources of information, we offer:

Recommendation 4: *Faculty should be aware of the professional and personal characteristics Adult students look for in their teachers.*

The professional characteristics include being knowledgeable, being well prepared and well organized, being able to communicate well, caring about students (as noted by Adult Undergraduates), being enthusiastic, and being challenging and demanding. Personal characteristics include: Caring about the student (identified by Graduate and Professional students), enjoying teaching, having a good attitude toward one's work, and having a good sense of humor.

Are these necessarily the characteristics of a good teacher? They are from the point of view of Adult students. Does this mean they represent the answer to what a faculty member must do to be a good teacher? It is possible that they do not, but they need to be considered since they are the views of those who are the consumers of education. Should faculty adopt the behaviors implicit in the characteristics? For reasons we will now describe, they should certainly be considered.

They should be considered because when students recognize these behaviors in faculty, they are more attentive to what is going on in class, and we believe that increased attention is related to increased learning. Translated into the faculty member's perspective, this means that adopting the behaviors increases how much attention students will spend on their studies. Students attend more carefully to teachers they admire and value, and that attentiveness results in increased learning. In other words, presenting the characteristics students look for in teaching means increasing the amount students will learn in class. It means faculty members displaying these attributes are more efficient teachers in the sense that students learn more from them per class hour.

But what, in fact, do these attributes mean? Being knowledgeable is an interesting characteristic. How do students (who, by definition, are not knowledgeable) recognize a knowledgeable teacher? McKeachie (1978) suggests that they cannot, but that they can and do use the term *knowledgeable* as a synonym for 'confidence in the teacher'. When an Undergraduate in an introductory class calls a professor 'knowledgeable', he is simply saying he has confidence in that person as a teacher.

Being enthusiastic is a more straight forward attribute. Enthusiasm can be expressed toward the material being taught (by showing that it is inherently interesting), toward the students (by evidencing pleasure at working with the class), and toward teaching (which happens when faculty appear to enjoy themselves as they teach). These forms of enthusiasm are evidenced by a teacher who is high energy, who is supportive, and who offers much opportunity for discussion with students about the topics at hand.

Caring about students is evidenced through being available to them to answer questions and consider their concerns. Though this is hardly a personal activity (after all, the issues discussed all deal with the subject matter in class), some students, particularly Undergraduates, see this kind of attention addressed toward them as evidence that they've made the proper decision electing the program they'd chosen.

We feel particularly strongly about two characteristics: caring about students, and enthusiasm. We suspect that these two may undergird the others since, for example, if one asks an Adult about how a faculty member dealt with students and expressed enthusiasm, the response might well include comments about knowledge, organization, preparation, and communication. This is understandable; to be seen as enthusiastic, a faculty member must know the material well enough and have communication skills sufficient to the tasks of communicating both content and positive affect. And, since the information taught and enthusiasm displayed is ultimately appreciated by students individually, appreciation of each student is a necessity. This, in turn, comes down to knowing one's students; if a faculty member knows his students, he is able to help them learn and ensure their needs are met.

Recommendation on Evaluation Strategies

We saw that important differences existed among groups of students: Graduate and Professional students preferred being evaluated on research and papers, and Undergraduates preferred group projects and being graded on the curve; Adults, regardless of college, were more like Graduate and Professional students than were Young Adults; and Professional students preferred being graded on tests only more often than did Graduate students. As a general rule, the older the students OR the further along students were in their educations, the more likely they were to want to be evaluated on their own accomplishments (e.g., papers and research projects) than in contrast with others (e.g., taking the same test as everyone else, and being graded on the curve).

Results of our study indicated much variability in the way Adult students view evaluation. Some Adults prefer to be evaluated on a project or paper (probably because they feel they will learn more from the activity or be better able to demonstrate how much they know and can do) while others would like to work at take home tests because they feel more competent with them — that is, tests allowing them to show what they know and could do in the virtual absence of time demands. Thus we offer:

Recommendation 5: *Faculty should allow Adult and more advanced students to select evaluation devices used to determine how much they know and what they can do.*

This is a good idea for a number of reasons beyond the time-constraint problem just described: Adult students generally have control over their lives and make their own decisions; and so they will select evaluation devices that both minimize disruptions to their lives and indicate how much they know and can do. If they were Young Adult Undergraduates, the motives driving their decision-making might cause the evaluation to be given short shrift; the fact is, though, that Adult students are not like this — they're enrolled in school precisely because they want to learn, and the evaluation device they select will allow them to demonstrate how much they have learned.

It is possible to produce a final examination that allows Adults to explore the ways in which the material they have been studying relates to the needs they have for the course they are finishing. That way is to have students design their own final project within constraints specified by the teacher, constraints addressing goals she has for the course, but, given the student's input, focused by the student on his own needs. Certainly, this takes more time for the instructor, and that is a serious drawback. However, the benefits to the student make the trade-off worthwhile.

This kind of evaluation begins with a meeting between the teacher and student so the teacher can be satisfied that the student understands the task and appreciates the goals the evaluation is to cover. If there is to be a specific final examination instrument, it needs to be drafted (by the student) and reviewed by both parties. The conversation at that time includes issues such as what the student will write and how the faculty member will examine the student's efforts.

Another approach to this kind of evaluation is to base a part of the final examination for each student on a class project. In this case, each student has a project to be completed two to three weeks before the term's end, and it is handed in on time. The instructor reads each student's paper and critiques it as usual: Good points are noted, problems are identified, and additional questions dealing with further applications of the student's findings are asked. The paper, with evaluative notes, is returned to the student along with a reminder that there will be a small number of questions on the final examination bearing on the paper. All students are told that their individual questions will address issues raised about their papers. And, indeed, each student's final examination has a series of common questions (questions asked of all students) and one or two addressed to each student individually.

In terms of work for the faculty member, the procedure requires little: The faculty member already reads and comments on each student's paper, and all that is required is a note or two about questions appropriate to the final. These questions might address errors the student made in the initial study ('You made the assumption that this variable was normally distributed and now you find reason to question whether that is reasonable. If you could do your study over, how would you deal with that problem?') or implications that might or might not have been considered ('You suggest that students become better problem solvers when they work at problem sets as members of a group. How could you find out whether that assertion is correct?').

There is an advantage to this technique that applies to all students, and another that is especially appropriate to Adult learners. In the former case, the advantage is that students gain additional benefit from all the work that went into the project because their attention is addressed to it in ways that encourage them to think further about what they have done. This contrasts with what students usually do: note the grade assigned to the paper and then file it away somewhere.

In the latter case, Adults tend to look to classes as sources of information and skill they need in order to address their educational goals. Assuming their projects address those same goals (i.e., they picked topics of interest to them), the evaluation procedure just described allows them additional opportunity to see how their work addresses their needs. When the issues raised by the faculty member on the paper are on target, the student can do nothing but learn more about the topic of interest to her.

There are other ways in which evaluation can be focused on Adults' needs. Students can be asked to identify problems in their own work experiences, say, that are approached by what they are learning in class, or the evaluation might take the form of a proposal for a study to attack a problem of particular interest (in this case, the teacher would read the proposal to see that the information taught in class was correctly applied in both analyzing the problem to be researched and conceptualizing an efficient approach to addressing the problem). A useful variation on the proposal theme is preparation of a 'manuscript' which follows journal format in that it includes an introduction (demonstrating knowledge of the literature and understanding of the problem to be solved), and a methods section (showing the student understands how to approach the problem). It may also be appropriate to manufacture data (this is done either by the student or the faculty member) so that additional skills such as analysis and interpretation can be demonstrated as well. In evaluating the manuscript, the faculty member may want to play the role of an editor and comment accordingly.

Skillful teachers also know that take home tests can be more demanding than in-class tests (that is, take home tests allow students to better exercise what they know and can do). For Adult and more advanced students, then, the choice among evaluation mechanisms is considerable, and the decision as to which one(s) to use should include student input.

Recommendation on Allocation of Time

Adult learners deal with a number of time-consuming issues. As noted earlier, they balance work and family responsibilities with class attendance and studying; and they do it by scheduling themselves almost to the minute. Only through efficient time allocation can they be students at the same time they are employees and family members.

Because of their tight schedules, disturbances such as having to deal with sick children, handling emergencies at work, or having to deal with unexpected school problems affect all parts of their lives. Thus we suggest:

Recommendation 6: *Communicate clear expectations for what students are to do, and state those expectations early so that students can plan their schedules with confidence.*

The logic for this recommendation is clear: Anything that stresses an already stressed schedule demands additional time and energy — if only to reschedule conflicts, arrange for a babysitter, find someone to cover at work, etc. One way faculty can protect against such things happening is through using a detailed syllabus, one specifying what is expected of students and when the expectations are to be realized. Spelling out times and dates for classes, tests, assignments, out-of-class activities, and so on, allows Adults to plan their schedules accordingly.

Spur-of-the-moment demands also cause problems (extending class an additional fifteen minutes so a topic can be completed; adding an additional assignment at the last minute), and avoiding these problems means minimizing the disruptions in Adults' lives and so increasing what they learn in school.

It is also true that unexpected opportunities arise (such as a prominent scholar coming to campus), and these should be made available to all students — whether Young Adult or Adult. However, these events are qualitatively different from the kinds of disturbances described in the preceding paragraph. Adult students feel very differently about having to reschedule for these kinds of activities because they can choose to participate or pass on the opportunity; in contrast, they are forced into rescheduling in the other case.

Finally, since it is true that one attribute of good teachers is that they appreciate students, it is not surprising that Adults appreciate faculty who recognize and accommodate to the occasional problem of a sick child, a nonfunctioning car, or an emergency at work that means being late or missing a class. One good way to deal with these problems is to ask the Adults involved what they propose as solutions to problems as they arise (since no one ever plans these things). 'When do you think you can have the paper in?' allows the student to regain control over what is otherwise an out-of-control situation, and it acknowledges that Adult Learners are, in fact, serious students who are concerned about both learning and doing a good job. Being punitive, and to a lesser extent, setting arbitrary deadlines in these situations, may simply aggravate an already difficult situation.

As noted in an earlier chapter, Young Adults may miss class often, and the reasons for their not being there may have little to do with their responsibilities. This is not true of Adults, however; they will attend all their classes because they want to learn and miss class only when it is truly impossible for them to attend. Faculty who understand this are valued by students and, more to the point of this chapter, are more likely to find that students profit from being in their classes.

Developmental Issues

Making a commitment to a career means more than deciding on a major. As we described earlier, this decision has both a cognitive component and an identity component to it, and it entails risks for both Adult and Young Adult students. These risks include whether they will be successful, whether they will be happy, and whether they will be accepted in the careers they choose.

Students who have not yet committed are generally, but not exclusively, Undergraduates; post-decision students are generally, but again not exclusively, Graduate students. We find Professional students to be somewhere between Undergraduates and Graduates. Medical students, for example, don't begin reaching the post-decision comfort with having committed to medicine until they've completed their basic sciences (studies covered during the first two years), and begin their clinical work during the third year.

This decision is much more than simply deciding what one wants to be. In addition to making the decision, the student must learn to be comfortable with it, to accept the idea that she *is* becoming a lawyer, or a social worker, or an engineer. It is for this reason that time elapses between a student's making a declaration of a major and realizing that she *really is* what she's set out to be.*

The declaration means not only learning the necessary knowledge and skills, but internalizing the ethic, the values, of members of the profession. In this way, the student *cum* professional learns to see the world from the perspective of members of the profession he is joining. Among other things, this means resolution to the problem of all the differing realities that can be used to view the world; by adopting the views of his profession, he has adopted one he can use to understand the world in which he finds himself.

Because students who have not yet made career commitments are less likely to see things from the same perspective as students who have committed, we make this suggestion for teaching pre-commitment students:

Recommendation 7: *Faculty need to be specific in working with pre-commitment students.*

These students want things concrete; use lots of examples, and provide demonstrations of how the theory taught looks when implemented in the classroom, courtroom, laboratory, hospital, and so on. Pre-commitment students want to be 'shown' how things work and this can be done through videos, demonstrations, case studies, and professionals describing their activities. At the same time, the values held by professionals in the area can be identified and described.

This is another way of saying pre-decision students want to be 'given truth' while post-decision students want to 'discover truth for themselves'. Pre-decision students resent open-ended, conjectural, activities; post-decision students resent being given the answers.

It is not easy for students to make the kind of decision we have been discussing. The decision is fraught with difficulties and so students need

* This can be easily shown. Ask anyone who has completed college to write down when they declared the major listed in their transcript. Next, ask them to write down when they first felt like a professional in that area. When we did this with practicing physicians, for example, we learned the declaration came early — most often during their undergraduate years — while they really didn't 'feel' like doctors until much later when someone else recognized that they were, indeed, doctors. In a case that is interesting because it came early, a pediatrician said it was during his third year of medical school when his patients called him 'doctor', and in another, more typical case, an internist told us it was during his first year of residency when he realized 'they could not throw anything at me in the emergency room that I couldn't handle'. 'They', of course, were the emergency room patients.

support while they are in the process of committing and becoming comfortable with themselves afterwards. Thus:

Recommendation 8:   *Faculty should be supportive.*

One way to do this is to be a role model of a person who has successfully made the same decision. In general, this means (i) showing how members of the profession deal with relativistic issues (i.e., how they function when their perspectives are different from others); (ii) showing both what members of the profession do and how they do those things; and (iii) showing how members of the profession deal with doubt and uncertainty. A successful faculty-as-role model will: Identify professional organizations and professional publications for students, encourage students to participate in activities such as attending professional meetings, sharing articles and research activities (less to provide information, more to demonstrate what members of the profession do), invite students to join in activities such as writing and research. Faculty members who do this show their areas of expertise to be both understandable and enjoyable.

Alan Knox (1986, pp. 132–134) offers some additional suggestions for creating a supportive physical and emotional environment. These include providing attractive facilities, presenting oneself as a person (e.g., see the earlier discussion of best liked teachers), and other suggestions we have noted already (e.g., facilitating participation, being available to students). In other words, the recommendations provided here are not independent of one another; they all work together, particularly in the process of providing support to students. Teachers who do these sorts of things will be recognized by students as 'responding to them as persons'.

Students who have made their commitments still need support, but they also need to learn the skills and knowledge they will need to be successful in the professions they have chosen. Thus:

Recommendation 9:   *Provide post-commitment students with opportunities to engage in professional activities.*

This means providing students with lots of background information (so they can see the milieu in which members of their profession work) as well as the concepts and principles they are to learn. Further, they should be given realistic problems to work on and be asked to solve them using appropriate professional tools, procedures, forms, vocabulary, etc. In addition, practicing professionals should be invited to the class to discuss students' solutions to the problems, and both the guests and the instructor need to respond to the students' efforts as professionals. Besides learning from these people, the opportunity to 'rub elbows' with them will provide students with less formal opportunities to see how professionals in 'their area' view the world. The contact will also help the students come to see themselves as professionals, too.

Institutional Recommendations

The preceding recommendations can be handled nicely by individual faculty members. There are other recommendations which can only be handled by institutions, however, because they require resources and authority individuals do not have. It is to those concerns we turn now.

Attending school is demanding, whether the Adult has just finished a bachelor's degree and is simply 'going straight through' or is on campus for the first time after graduating from high school twenty years earlier. These demands — which have already been met and handled by others — must nevertheless be met and handled by each person as they encounter them. Knowledge that others have dealt with them successfully in the past is often little consolation to someone in the midst of preparing for exams, raising children, and living on a minimal budget. And so we recommend:

Recommendation 10: *Institutions should establish and maintain support groups for Adult students.*

People in support groups have something professionals — no matter how qualified and how well-intentioned — do not have: They have the credibility that comes with having dealt with the problem at hand. Thus a group of Adult parents of little children might not only provide each other with empathic support, they can also share emotional and experiential resources and offer suggestions on how to deal with problems (e.g., by swapping babysitting). Such groups can be the difference between a stressed Adult remaining in school and dropping out.

These meetings should, of course, be held at regular times and in the same location each time. This is because regular meetings are easier to fit into a schedule. The university should also arrange for meeting facilities both because the university is a central location for Adult students and because it is easier for the university to do this than the Adults (it saves them time).

Similarly, the university is in a better position to know who to invite (it has a roster of all Adult learners enrolled) and it has access to other resources (counselors, for example, as the group might find them useful) that are either unknown to the students or otherwise unavailable.

One reason Adult students who have been away from school for a long time are stressed is that they believe their academic skills have deteriorated (they might not have used algebra for years) or skills are now required that were unheard of when they were students (many Adults returning to school are not computer literate). Thus we suggest:

Recommendation 11: *Institutions should offer refresher/remedial courses covering skills and knowledge necessary for success in college level courses.*

Though this recommendation bears more on Adults who will also be Undergraduates, some people returning for graduate degrees will appreciate them as well. Such courses will not carry credit toward graduation, of course, but they may well provide students with something more important: Successfully completing a course in an area such as mathematics, computers, or composition may provide Adults with the confidence they need to enroll as full-time students.

In addition, a student who completes such a course has a further resource which may be valuable later: a faculty member to turn to in the event of a problem in mathematics, computer science, or writing. As we have implied on several occasions, knowing that one is well-regarded by a faculty member contributes considerably to a student's success.

The same kinds of benefits can accrue from courses designed to develop study practices that either were nonexistent or have deteriorated from lack of use. And so a university that wishes to enroll Adults should:

Recommendation 12: *Establish a program for enhancing students' study skills.*

This kind of program might be both formal and informal. Formal offerings might appear at the beginning of the semester and run for a brief period of time with the purpose of helping students learn to use computerized library search procedures, or after mid-terms for students who suddenly realize their studying and test-taking skills are inadequate.

Informal offerings might be established to address the *ad hoc* needs of students with special problems. In this case, the student would arrange to meet with an instructor for a brief series of sessions to work on the specific problem.

But more importantly, the instructor may help the Adult determine if his abilities are adequate, and, if they are not, whether they can be remediated. Such an evaluation would consider how much time and energy is required to accomplish the needed changes.

Child care is a better name than 'day care' since the services Adult students require in this area may also extend into the night. This would be the case if evenings and weekends were given over to classes, outside employment, library research, or studying. In any event, we recommend:

Recommendation 13: *Institutions should establish child care facilities to be open for extended hours.*

Arranging for child care is a major problem for many Adults. First, someone must be found to take care of the children, and, second, this must be more than custodial care for children old enough to profit from pre-school. Third, there is the matter of transporting children to the child care center and picking them up afterwards — an issue that involves both scheduling time and the use of the family car. All these issues appear in the schedules of Adults who are also parents. But without these facilities, Adults' abilities to attend school are constrained indeed. In other words, the presence of affordable day care on campus addresses an important demand on the lives of Adults who are also parents.

Summary

Adult learners are a highly variable lot: They range in ages, interests, and the goals they have for their educations. Nonetheless, they share similarities bearing on how successful they will be at realizing their educational goals. In this chapter, we have cast recommendations addressing needs implicit in some of those similarities in the hope that they might contribute to the education of Adult learners.

Chapter 7

Epilogue

Looking Back

When our research group met to review the last draft of this book, we talked about the fact that three years have passed since we began the efforts described here. We looked at each other and wondered, 'How did the time pass so quickly?'

Introduction

If the three years passed quickly for us, they must have flown by for the Young Adults and Adults we interviewed. Three years is a long time in a person's educational career; a person can go through law school, begin and complete a master's degree or a doctorate, or all but finish a bachelor's or medical program. As we finished the efforts presented in the preceding chapters, we thought again about the thirteen people we'd interviewed earlier. We wondered how their lives were progressing, and we wondered, too, whether their experiences over the past three years supported the findings of our study. And so we set out to contact these people for a second round of interviews.

We were unable to contact one of the thirteen, *Daniel (YA, G)*, who had completed his master's degree in Aerospace Science and had taken a job with a large Southern California firm concerned with the space program. Though we were sorry we could not talk with him, we thought about his observation, three years ago, that he had just recently reached the point where he could see where he 'fit in' in the world, and that was in Aerospace Science. We would have liked to learn how the experiences he is having now squared with what he had expected.

Young Adults

Young Adults Revisited

We expected to see the Young Adults gaining the kinds of experiences the Adults already had and, indeed, that is exactly what happened. *Rhonda (YA,G)*, for example, reports having grown both personally and professionally. In general terms, she is less naive, more sure of herself, more at peace with herself and the 'significant others' in her life.

More specifically, *Rhonda* attributes much of her growth to experiences she has had as a student. She agrees with her mother's observation that she will have an easier time raising her children because of her schooling (*Rhonda* is currently enrolled in an infant development program).

In fact, *Rhonda* plans on returning to school at some point after she finishes her master's degree and has been out working for a while. She wants to be more financially secure before she commits to school again when she returns to work on a degree in either speech pathology or occupational therapy.

The kinds of experiences Young Adults have in the process of becoming adults are highly varied. *Charles (YA,U)* experienced this variability both through school and work he did during the summers for the Boy Scout camp serving this part of the country. He learned problem solving skills in his engineering courses, he told us, and about people in the developmental psychology classes he took. Hearing him talk, however, we suspect that he learned a lot about problem solving involving people during the summers as he assumed more and more responsibilities at the Scout camp, responsibilities underscoring for him his belief that the world is more complex than he had thought previously. Though *Charles* was never without self-confidence, his self-confidence is now based on experiences he had not enjoyed earlier, the same experiences providing him with insights and skills he needs to deal with the diversity of people and problems he will encounter in the future. He also reports letting fewer minor problems bother him. Still hard working and outspoken, he describes himself as more altruistic — more committed to doing things for others.

Charles is currently a senior in engineering and anticipates working on a master's degree in environmental engineering after graduation. The kind of education he will enjoy next year is qualitatively different from what he has experienced in the past because, while he had a general interest in engineering three years ago, he is now more specific about both what he wants from his master's degree and the kinds of learning experiences he expects. In the former case, he has a better idea of what it is to be 'an engineer'; the idea of being an engineer has a degree of clarity to it that it did not have in 1988. In the latter case, he talked about instruction in which he would be more directly involved with his professors. We believe this instruction will allow him to observe, first hand, the values, the ethics, and the approach to the world held by engineers of the variety he aspires to be. In other words, he currently has an idea of what it means to be an engineer, but he has not yet completed defining his professional identity.

Five years from now he would like to have finished his master's degree, have a family, and work for a regulatory agency — probably more in the line of designing regulatory procedures or being a manager than being an inspector.

An important attribute of Young Adults (and also Adult Undergraduates) is the need to be validated as people. *Billie Jo (YA,U)* describes her life now in terms suggesting she has matured enough so she no longer has this need. Because of her experiences at the University, she has learned to work in groups, and this has contributed to her self-confidence. Hearing her comments on groups and her description of herself as 'secure in who I am — and strong', we wonder whether the growth she described is simply part of becoming an adult, a growth that occurred in parallel to her academic achievements.

The fact is she did learn how to function in groups and that learning, combined with what she had learned about chemistry, allowed her to describe herself in our recent interview as professional, competent, and independent. *Billie Jo* presents herself as a successful young professional woman.

We reminded *Billie Jo* that a goal she had three years ago for her education was to hold an intelligent conversation at some time. Her response reflected both the confidence she had in herself and the sense of humor she has always had. 'I hold intelligent conversations daily', she noted.

Billie Jo graduated from college and married during the past three years. She now works for an engineering consulting firm doing environmental engineering in California. Five years from now she expects to have continued growing in terms of both her profession and in her relationships with her family.

Martin (YA,P) graduated from law school and took a job with a large law firm in Wisconsin. Three years ago, he believed he could 'change the world', an expectation he now characterizes as naive. Based on what he has learned since then, he now sees that things can change, but that change happens slowly in part because the world is a broader, more diverse place than he had previously thought. We see his adopting this perspective as consistent with his having reached a post-formal operations level of cognitive development. He appears to understand, for example, that, since not everyone views the world as he does, making the changes he might like to see requires the efforts of many people.

Martin believes his experiences on campus were not reflective of the world he finds himself in now; the University environment, he felt, was conservative. This is an interesting observation both because of what it says about *Martin* and what it says about how he views the University. Concerning *Martin*, the comment may well reflect the fact that, as a Young Adult, his view of the world was not enriched by the experiences of life;

had he been ten years older when he attended law school, for example, he might report something very different. Concerning his view of the University, the conservatism he reports might well be considered flaming liberalism by another student.

The last Young Adult we talked with was *Britt (YA,P)* who was a beginning medical student when we began the research reported here. Like *Martin*, she went directly from high school to college to professional school; unlike him, she is currently one year away from graduation. During the next twelve months, she contemplates both marriage and beginning a residency in obstetrics and gynecology.

Britt reports becoming stronger for the experience of going to medical school (she describes having her ego 'stamped on daily', taking a large amount of responsibility, and seeing a lot). In the last two years, her work with physicians and residents allowed her to see first hand the ways in which physicians view themselves, their worlds, and other people. These experiences, we believe, allowed her to better visualize the kind of professional she wished to become. We believe, in other words, that her decision for obstetrics and gynecology was not simply a declaration of intent to limit her practice, but rather a statement of how she feels about patients in general, women in particular, and how she feels about the way she wants to provide medical care for them.

She currently sees herself as reliable, dependable, friendly, and because of her medical school experiences, having an increased dedication and commitment to study. Some of these terms are those reflective of having strengthened the commitment she made to medicine years ago, a strengthening that became possible only through seeing physicians at work and trying out for herself the kinds of things she saw them doing.

Five years from now she anticipates being married, having a family, and specializing in the practice of obstetrics and gynecology.

Summary

Clearly, these Young Adults have grown, and their growth is attributable to both life experiences and education. Concerning the life experiences, we believe that these six people are now more like the seven Adults than they were three years ago. And, while they are similar in this regard, there are still differences.

Adults

Adults Revisited

The Adults told us they had experienced less growth than did the Young Adults due to the fact that they were not just starting out; they had earlier

experienced the kinds of things the Young Adults were just now reporting. We suspect that because the impact of education is both less dramatic
and more expected than issues associated with growing from eighteen to
twenty-four years of age, the Adults had overlooked their considerable
personal and professional growth.

We were not surprised when *Jerry (A,P)* told us he had grown little
over the last three years; he is pretty much the same as he was then
because, he believes, much of the growing one does takes place during
one's early twenties. 'Then, unless you have something major happen,
you continue to grow in the same way. You just keep goin' down the
road'. Because *Jerry* was admitted to the Montana bar, we know he picked
up skills and knowledge over the past three years sufficient to pass a
demanding test. These experiences (both going to law school and becoming a member of the Montana legal community) contributed importantly
to who *Jerry* is and how he thinks of himself; these are no mean accomplishments. But more to the point of this discussion, being a lawyer reflects a perspective and an ethic — important aspects of his identity.
Consequently, though *Jerry* believes he had grown little in law school, we
disagree, and we are confident in our analysis of him because of his observation: 'It [law school] opened my eyes to the realities of life in the
profession'.

Jerry believes there is much left to learn about the law. When we
asked what he wanted to be like five years from now, his observation was
that he wants to be well schooled in the law, and that he learns something
new every day. We would only add that this implies that his identity as
a lawyer is not yet complete.

Jerry has his son with him most of the time. He also anticipates that,
five years from now, he will be remarried and continue to have a good
relationship with his son.

Robert (A,P) also completed a professional education during the last
three years, though his graduation was from medical school. Like *Jerry*, he
also reported growing less than the younger students though, again like
Jerry, he in fact realized tremendous growth in skill and knowledge, and
a sense of what it means to be a physician.

Robert is now a psychiatry resident. In a phrase, residents learn their
specialties by 'practicing medicine under supervision' and that is exactly
what *Robert* does. He has 'his' patients, and he is responsible for their well
being though he works under the eye of faculty members. He is learning
to apply what he has already learned as well as what he is currently studying, and he does all this within the intellectual framework provided by the
medical problems presented by the patients he deals with. In identifying
his patients' problems, collecting information bearing on those problems,
proposing solutions, and testing those solutions by referring them to his
teachers as well as trying them on the patients, *Robert* is, in fact, incorporating psychiatric medicine into his personal and professional identity.

Not only do his efforts help patients with their problems, but the successes and failures he encounters change the person he is.

Amber (A,P) also completed law school and now works for the Tax Division of the Justice Department. There are thirty to thirty-five other lawyers in her group.

Amber described personal as well as professional changes occurring to her over the past three years. She is much more personally and professionally secure and comfortable than previously, and she says she is now better able to see the 'big picture' and so is better able to decide what should be the focus of her attention. Law school was important to the changes she has made in her life because it presented her with an entirely new set of challenges; it challenged her in ways that she had never considered before. We take this as evidence that she considered and began adopting the ethic and values associated with being a lawyer.

Amber's plans for the next five years are ill-defined. Though she reports not having thought very far in the future, she has made a four-year commitment to the federal government.

Steve (A,G) also echoes the theme of little change over the past three years. He told us he has the same goals and is the same person, that attending graduate school has changed him little. He is currently completing work on his dissertation. Five years from now he plans on being a professor of marketing; he expects to be teaching, doing research, and being involved in the community. Like many of the Adults on campus, he hopes leaving school and taking a fulltime job will also mean more money.

We were as interested in what *Steve* (as well as the other non-Undergraduates) did not say about their educations as what he did tell us. In addition to comments bearing on the law, medicine, and graduate school, they made no observations about the people who taught them. This is, we believe, because they see their teachers more as people, less as providers of skill and knowledge — a perspective deriving from the view of both Graduate and Professional students that good teachers validate the subject matter they're teaching and not the students who study it. Had they been Undergraduates, they would have been more likely to comment on their teachers.

Marlys (A,G) had a second child during the past three years and is now, in addition to caring for her babies, finishing her dissertation in psychology. She reports being calmer and more self assured now than previously. When she begins working (after her children start school), her education will have enabled her to do what she wants to do.

The fact that she had her second child during the past three years reflects the reality that while school is important to Adults, it is not the only item on their agendas. Marlys' having a baby while in graduate school simply underscores the points we have described earlier in Chapters 2 and 3.

Marlys reports 'feeling more like a professional' since she has accomplished most of her goals. We believe that feeling like a professional is more a function of her internalizing the knowledge and skill of a psychologist than a reflection of having completed courses and passed tests. If it were otherwise, she would not be concerned with which courses she was required to take, for example; she would see her course work as simply hurdles to be jumped. But that is not the case as she saw her graduate work as being 'out of control' because she had little to say about what she studied. Now that she has reached a point where all that remains is completing her dissertation, she sees her current life as more 'in control' — she has more to say about what she will do and when she will do it.

We wonder about whether the 'out of control' description may not have reflected pressures on *Marlys* beyond what was happening at school. We noted earlier that Adults deal with a myriad of pressures including being parents and spouses as well as students, and that each of these roles impinges on each other role. From this perspective, *Marlys* demonstrates that the pressures experienced by Adult learners continue; they are not unique to a given part of the student's career.

Five years from now, *Marlys* anticipates that both of her children will be in school and she will be working, probably in a mental health facility.

Three years ago, *Jimmy* was a 'high energy' 40-year-old Undergraduate. Though he had expected to be finished with his program by now, a change in major prolonged his stay at the University. For both personal and academic reasons, he decided to change from pre-med to social studies education. He says he will student teach in the spring and then be finished.

Jimmy is pleased with his career change. Because of what he learned in taking various courses and what he knows about himself, he feels a sense of accomplishment. He is more confident in himself as a student now than he was three years ago: he is more productive, things come easier to him, and his change in major made him want to study more. In five years, *Jimmy* wants to teach in the public schools and then work on a doctorate.

Naomi was a 47-year-old who became an Undergraduate after living in a variety of places and holding a variety of jobs. During the past three years, she and her husband (who was also a student) have both graduated and moved to the Pacific Northwest. They moved there because her husband was offered an excellent job. She is currently looking for a permanent position. In the meantime, she works as an accompanist for an 84-year-old cellist. Compared to three years ago, she is still gregarious, intense, curious; and she also describes herself as more creative, more knowledgeable about herself, and tired — but still high energy.

Because of her college experiences, she describes herself as more knowledgeable about academia, and more confident in herself academically because of the feedback she got from her teachers. It is interesting that an Undergraduate referred to interactions with teachers, and the interaction provided information about *her*. We recall that Undergraduates want teachers to validate them as people, and that is exactly what happened to *Naomi*; her confidence in herself academically is due to what her teachers told her.

In fact, that confidence (and thus the impact of her teachers) had to have some bearing on her thinking about returning to school in the future to work on a Ph.D. in linguistics. She would then like to teach at the college level.

Summary

In other words, Adult themes play out here (*Marlys'* having to balance family and school work, for example) as do some themes attributable to cognitive and identity development (as in the cases of Steve and Robert). And finally, there are themes that are attributable to college (such as *Naomi's* being validated by teachers she had had and *Jimmy's* being validated by a change in major).

What is most interesting, though, is the general feeling among the Adults that what they had experienced was somehow less impressive than what the Young Adults enjoyed. Without a doubt, the Young Adults participated in life experiences which were dramatic (because they were new to them) and important contributors to their maturation (because of the impact they had on their lives). But then, the experiences of the Adults were also important though for different reasons. The fact is that the experiences of the past three years were invaluable to the thirteen students, informative to us, and, we sincerely hope, interesting and useful to you.

A Final Thought

We were surprised and pleased with the number of Young Adults and Adults who will further their educations. In some cases, that meant heading off in a new direction (such as *Naomi's* interest in linguistics) while in others it meant additional graduate education either now (*Charles*) or in the future (*Rhonda* and *Jimmy*). In still others (*Martin, Britt, Jerry, Robert,* and *Amber*), it meant continuing education in the professions. In all cases, it means these people will be Adult learners whose needs are documented in this volume and elsewhere, and whose teachers should find useful the recommendations we have provided in the preceding chapter as well as those made by others.

Appendix A: Methodology

The findings we report in this book are the result of a survey we conducted of Young Adults and Adults who were full-time students on campus at the University of North Dakota during the Spring semester, 1988–89 academic year. This appendix describes the materials and methods used in that survey with particular reference to the survey instrument, the sampling plan, data collection, and analytic and interpretive strategies.

Survey Instrument

The instrument was based on a review of the general adult education literature as well as specific literatures concerned with more limited questions (e.g., the Bureau of the Census' Current Population Studies concerned with higher education). We reviewed these materials and identified those topics we wished the instrument to cover.

In addition, we added questions designed to collect information useful in interpreting respondents' answers to the first questions, information including reasons for attending our University. We added questions on other aspects of students' lives (such as domestic responsibilities and employment) and university services (including parking, registration, etc.) that do not impact directly on quality of education, but have a bearing on it nevertheless.

We used a combination of forced-choice and open-ended questions, with the decision as to which type to use being determined by the nature of the issue the question was to address. In collecting certain kinds of attitude measures, for example, respondents simply selected from among available options while for other kinds of questions (such as how many hours do you spend studying each week?) brief answers were requested. In yet another kind of question (e.g., describe the most serious obstacle you have had to overcome in getting your education) more extended answers were requested. In all cases, we offered respondents opportunities

Table 17: Outline of topics covered in the survey

Background information (including demographics)	Family history Current family situation Current employment situation
Educational history	High school education College education history Current enrollment
Views on aspects of teaching and learning	Preferred instructional style Best and worst teachers Deterrents and obstacles Personal academic strengths and weaknesses Preferred evaluation strategies

to provide answers that were complete, brief, and easily coded.

Members of our group field tested the draft instrument by using it to interview volunteers from different segments of the student body (see sample selection below). The students 'talked their way through the questions' so we could better appreciate how they understood and interpreted each of the questions. Similarly, if the students did not understand what we wanted, or found a question ambiguous, the interviewer was available to provide paraphrased prompts or clarifications. This procedure allowed us to identify and then clarify ambiguities and otherwise make the questions more straightforward. The final form of the instrument is presented in Appendix B.

The revised instrument, along with the sampling plan and analytic strategy described below, were then passed on to the University's Institutional Review Board for approval. Once approval was granted, the sample was drawn and the study begun.

Sampling Plan

The instrument produced was mailed to a stratified random sample (Cochran, 1977) of the student body at the University during the Spring semester of the 1987–88 academic year. We considered the following issues in developing the sampling plan:

Age Since we were interested in traditional age students as well as those who were older, and since we used the definition in the literature of age 25 or beyond as defining the latter group, we divided students into two groups: Young Adult (age 24 and younger) and Adult (age 25 and older). In this study, the categories apply to students regardless of whether they are enrolled as undergraduates or are pursuing post-graduate studies.

College We also suspected that differences among students could

Table 18: Population stratum sizes, sample sizes, and response rates

College	Age Group Young Adult	Adult	Total
Undergraduate			
Stratum Size	6777	1667	8444
Sample Size	96	97	193
Responses	61	66	127
Response rate	64 %	68 %	66 %
Graduate			
Stratum Size	198	756	954
Sample size	98	98	196
Responses	56	78	134
Response rate	57 %	80 %	68 %
Professional			
Stratum size	180	230	410
Sample size	100	98	198
Responses	68	74	142
Response rate	68 %	76 %	72 %
Total			
Stratum size	7155	2653	9808
Sample size	294	293	587
Responses	185	218	403
Response rate	63 %	74 %	69 %

be attributed to their colleges, and so we further divided the population into Undergraduate (regardless of major), Graduate (again, regardless of major), and Professional (limited to the colleges of law and medicine).

In short, we divided the students at the University into six strata (as described in Table 18). Note that we limited ourselves to those students enrolled full-time at the University — we did not consider persons who took classes on a part-time basis, or those enrolled in continuing education.

Sample Size

In questions with a yes-or-no answer, we felt a 10 per cent difference between two groups (i.e., two of the six strata just defined) would be about the smallest that would still be large enough to be 'educationally important'. Consequently, we decided our sample size would have to be sufficiently large to render such a difference statistically significant at alpha = 0.05. Given the worst possible case (the situation where variability was maximal, that is, one group said yes 55 per cent of the time, the other 45 per cent), we expected to need 50 persons from each stratum.

Now it is true that not everyone who receives a questionnaire in the mail answers it, and so we sampled more than fifty persons per stratum. Conservatively assuming a response rate of 50 per cent (indeed, we expected a 67–75 per cent return), we randomly selected one hundred persons from each stratum. This strategy meant that a 50 per cent response rate would allow us to declare a 10 per cent difference statistically significant at alpha = 0.05 while better response rates gave us the choice of either smaller differences being significant at this same alpha level, or demanding the same 10 per cent difference, but with a smaller associated probability, e.g., 0.01. We chose the latter option: *Throughout this book, 'statistically significant' means the test statistic had a probability of* $\alpha < 0.01$. We chose this approach both because we considered the educational importance of differences of less than 10 per cent to be minimal, and because using the lower alpha level reduced the likelihood of type I (false positive) errors when much hypothesis testing is to be done. The 'educational importance' of 10 per cent will be again considered when responses to open-ended questions are described.

Since our goal was to estimate parameters for strata, we elected to sample the same number of persons (100) from each stratum. This strategy allowed us to produce estimates of approximately the same precision for all groups as well as allowing us to produce campuswide population estimates.

The sampling frame (the names of everyone eligible to participate) was provided by the University upon our study's approval by the Institutional Review Board. We used a random number table to select respondents from the stratified list of those eligible.

Data Collection

Each person whose name was selected received a signed, personal letter from us exactly one week before the survey instrument arrived. Besides describing the study and soliciting participation, the letter pointed out that data would be handled confidentially, and also implied that the decision to *not* participate was certainly up to each respondent.

Some letters came back as undeliverable (e.g., address unknown, no longer enrolled), and we replaced those persons with others drawn randomly from the corresponding strata. Because these people were unavailable to us, we considered they had been included in the sampling frame in error.

A second personal letter accompanied each survey instrument as did a self-addressed, stamped envelope for use in returning the completed questionnaire. Each envelope had a number on it to identify those respondents who did not return questionnaires. Specifically, as we received each questionnaire, it was separated from its envelope and prepared for data entry while the envelope's number was noted so the respondent would not be sent reminders. We sent reminder letters (to be described shortly) to anyone whose number was not checked off. Note that anonymity was preserved because the number on the envelope was not transcribed onto the questionnaire and thus did not accompany the data in its analysis.

Two reminder letters were sent out, one two weeks after the instrument, and the second a week after that (i.e., three weeks after the initial instrument). The last letter speculated that the respondent might have misplaced the original questionnaire, and so a fresh one (with a second stamped return envelope) was included. Reminder letters also appear in Appendix B.

Using this procedure, 403 of the 597 questionnaires were returned and usable (see Table 18) and so our overall response rate was 69 per cent. All but a handful came in within five weeks of the initial mailing, and the few that came in later were added to the sample.

Data entry was a two-step procedure with answers to forced-choice questions entered on the mainframe while responses to open-ended questions were entered on a microcomputer database to be printed out and analyzed later. This procedure allowed us to examine both varieties of data quickly and easily.

Analytic Strategy

In all cases, graphical procedures were used to explore the data before inferential techniques were employed (Chambers *et al.*, 1982; and du Toit *et al.*, 1986). The charts and graphs so produced allowed us to better conceptualize patterns of responses and so more intelligently cast hypotheses to be tested. Because of the quantity of questions covered in the survey instrument, we were concerned about the large number of hypotheses to be tested and the implications this carried for type I errors. To simultaneously reduce the number of hypothesis tests and consider the fact that our dependent measures were correlated, we employed multivariate analyses of variance (MANOVA's) with Age and College — the stratification variables — as main effects.

In other words, we looked at differences among the various Age-and-College populations using the MANOVA. In the case of Age, this was straight forward: Any observed significance had to be due to differences between Young Adult and Adult students. In examining the Colleges (Undergraduate, Graduate, and Professional), we were interested in two comparisons: The Undergraduates versus the combined Graduate and Professional students, and the Graduate versus the Professional students. Using *a priori* planned orthogonal contrasts in this way, we avoided testing the College main effect and moved directly the questions of interest to us.

In the event of significant Age-by-College interactions, we planned to use simple effects and contrast-contrast comparisons to tease out the sources of the significance. As it turned out, interactions almost never appeared — an important finding in our study.

In all cases, when significance was found, we used *profile analysis* (Morrison, 1976) to identify those dependent variable(s) responsible for the observed significance. Briefly, this meant checking to see if the differences involved all the dependent measures, and, if they did not, searching for those which could be cast out as not contributing. There is a third aspect to profile analysis (testing to find out whether all dependent variables have equal means), though we elected not to use it. Instead, we first computed an estimate of the population mean for each variable based on a stratified random sample (Cochran, 1977) and then used a scree test to identify clusters of dependent variables with approximately the same value. Using a scree test meant ranking the means and then plotting the value of each mean by the variable's rank order and then looking for discontinuities — that is, places where variables adjacent to one another in the rank ordering had markedly discrepant mean values (see Slotnick, 1982). This allowed us to look at large numbers of dependent measures simultaneously rather than in the smaller sets created for the profile analyses.

We elected not to use standard-error-based hypothesis testing procedures in evaluating responses to open-ended questions (e.g., list the three things you liked best about the best teacher you ever had) because the specification of a number (3) built statistical and measurement constraints into the data (i.e., there may have been more than three attributes, but respondents were not allowed to list them, and there may be attributes the respondents had not considered). We were concerned that these constraints would affect the sampling distributions of the test statistics in unknown ways.

In these cases, we employed a combination of graphical and other procedures in analyzing the data (Slotnick, 1982). First, the responses were categorized and tabulations made of the number of persons selecting each category of response. Lastly, diagrams called 'stars' or 'asters' were created to display the proportions of persons selecting each category (see Chambers *et al.*, 1983, and du Toit *et al.*, 1986). If two groups of subjects (e.g., Young Adults and Adults) differed by more than 10 per cent *viz.* one of these measures, we considered the difference large enough to be 'educationally important' and thus worthy of further examination.

Interpretation

Four sources of information were tapped in interpreting the results of the analyses just described. The first two are quite conventional: Literature reviews on students (primarily on Adult learners), and the developmental psychology of adulthood, particularly cognitive and identity development.

The third source of information was answers to questionnaire items other than the ones under immediate consideration. This means that because we took a broad look at students, we were able to interpret answers to one question in terms of answers to others, an attack ensuring that the descriptions developed were internally consistent.

Finally, the fourth source of interpretive information was the students themselves. After the initial survey had been completed, we identified two or three students in each of the six strata for indepth interviews (though the students need not have participated in the study). These thirteen students (introduced in Chapter 1 on adult learning) were either already known to us or were nominated by deans or department chairs as examples of students at that age (either Young Adult or Adult) and college (Undergraduate, Graduate, or Professional). We began the interviews by taking an educational history from each student and then providing the student with survey results to interpret. Why, we asked, would students in the same age group and college as you report thus-and-such? The answers were both interesting and enlightening and are reported here along with the statistical findings based on the survey and the previously described sources of interpretive information. Note, though, that the names (and some other identifying characteristics) have been changed to protect their anonymity.

Summary

We wished to employ survey and analytic strategies which simultaneously provided maximal information at minimal threat to either the internal or external validity of the study. These constraints meant eschewing large sample sizes (because differences would then risk being statistically significant but educationally unimportant), testing sets of dependent measures simultaneously, and examining particular dependent variables only if *prima facie* evidence of differences were found.

There were also circumstances where non-standard-error based hypothesis testing was done (identifying clusters of variables and analyzing data from open-ended questions) because the assumptions required for more formal procedures could not be supported. In those cases, essentially graphical procedures were used.

Finally, we interpreted our findings with reference to both the existing literature and what students on campus had to say.

Appendix B: Survey Instrument and Letters to Respondents

The six-page questionnaire we sent out was printed on both sides of a sheet 25.5 inches wide and 11 inches high. The sheet was creased so that when the right-hand third was folded in toward the center, and the left-hand third folded on top of it, the questionnaire was a standard 8.5″ × 11″ in size. When respondents opened it, they found page 1 on the front, pages 2, 3, and 4 on the inside, and pages 5 and 6 on the back.

As noted in Appendix A, the respondent letters were all personally addressed and signed. The letters we've included here are addressed to a hypothetical student; we've included a name simply so the format for each of the letters can be seen.

Appendix B: Survey Instrument and Letters to Respondents

ADULT LEARNER CONSULTING GROUP
QUESTIONNAIRE

Please answer each question on this form in the space provided and return the completed questionnaire in the accompanying self-addressed envelope.

On behalf of the Consulting Group, thank you for taking the time to complete and return this form.

Mary Helen Pelton, Ed.D.
Assistant Dean
Division of Continuing Education

BACKGROUND INFORMATION

1. What is your age? _____

2. What is your gender?

   _____ male

   _____ female

3. How many **older** brothers and sisters do you have? _____

4. How many **younger** brothers and sisters do you have? _____

5. What kind of program are you enrolled in at UND?

   _____ Undergraduate

   _____ Graduate

   _____ Professional (Law, Medicine)

6. What is your current marital status?

   _____ Single, never married

   _____ Married

   _____ Separated or divorced

   _____ Widowed

7. If you are married, what was your age at the time of your current marriage? _____

8. If you are divorced or widowed, what was your age at the time of this change in your marital status? _____

9. Do you hold a job concurrently while going to school?

   Yes _____   No _____

   If yes, how many hours do you work at that job in a week? _____

10. Do you have domestic responsibility for children living at home?

    Yes _____   No _____

    If yes, do you share these responsibilities with another adult?

    Yes _____   No _____

11. About how many hours a week do you devote to housework and/or childcare? _____

12. Please list all **full-time** jobs you have held. List the most recent first:

Job/Occupation	Dates of Employment
	to
	to
	to
	to
	to
	to

EDUCATIONAL HISTORY

13. What kind of community did you live in at the time you graduated from or last attended high school? (Put a check in front of the appropriate category)

_____ Rural

_____ Town Population less than 2500

_____ Town Population 2500-9999

_____ Town Population 10,000-99,999

_____ City Population over 100,000

14. What state/province did you live in at the time you graduated from or last attended high school?

_____

15. Which of the following statements best describes your pre-college education? (Put a check in the appropriate category)

I have a high school diploma _____

I received a GED (high school equivalence degree) _____

Other — Please explain _____

_____

_____

16. Please list the colleges/universities you have attended. Begin with your current enrollment at the University of North Dakota:

Name of College	Dates of Attendance	Degree Earned if any	Date of Degree
	to		
	to		
	to		
	to		
	to		
	to		

17. Was your education ever interrupted (e.g., did you take time off or drop out at any time)?

Yes _____ No _____

If yes, please indicate why _____

_____

18. Please read the following list and put a check in front of each statement that applies to your current enrollment in college.

_____ preparing to begin first occupation

_____ changing occupations or careers

_____ gain new skills and knowledge for my present occupation

_____ career enhancement (e.g., to take on new responsibilities)

_____ life enhancement

_____ change in life situation — Please describe _____

_____

_____ other — Please explain _____

_____

19. Why did you choose to attend UND? _____

_____

20. When do you anticipate completing your current studies? _____

21. How many credit hours are you carrying this semester? _____

22. Approximately how many hours per week do you spend studying and preparing for class? _____

23. Approximately how many hours per week do you spend in class as a student (including field experience and laboratory)? _____

24. What degree, if any, will you receive at the time you complete your studies?_____

TEACHING AND LEARNING EXPERIENCES

Think of the **best college teacher** you have ever had so that you can describe that individual as a teacher and as a person.

25. List three characteristics of that instructor's **teaching** that you felt contributed most to your learning

a. _____

b. _____

c. _____

26. List three **personal** attributes of the instructor that you felt contributed most to your learning:

a. _____

b. _____

c. _____

27. What grade(s) did you receive in the instructor's course? _____

Think of the **least effective college teacher** you have ever had so that you can describe that individual as a teacher and as a person.

28. List three characteristics of that instructor's **teaching** you felt hindered your learning:

    a. _____

    b. _____

    c. _____

29. List three **personal** attributes of the instructor you felt hindered your learning:

    a. _____

    b. _____

    c. _____

30. What grade(s) did you receive in the instructor's course? _____

31. Examine the following list of teaching/learning strategies. Put a (+) in front of each strategy you like, and put a (−) in front of each you do not like. Put a (u) in front of each strategy that is **unfamiliar** to you. If you are neutral or have no opinion, please leave the space blank.

    _____ lectures with discussion

    _____ seminars at which students present papers and discuss them

    _____ seminars at which students' own relevant work experiences are discussed

    _____ courses that have required writing assignments

    _____ practical projects

    _____ analysis of research studies

    _____ case studies

    _____ use of simulation

    _____ individual projects

    _____ group projects

    _____ computer assisted instruction

    _____ small study groups

    _____ student participation in designing courses

32. Examine the following list of strategies for evaluating a student's work. Put a plus (+) in front of each strategy you like. Put a minus (−) in front of each you do not like. Put a (u) in front of each strategy that is **unfamiliar** to you. If you are neutral or have no opinion, please leave the space blank.

    _____ assessment by examination

    _____ assessment by assignment in addition to examinations

    _____ assessment based on research and term papers

    _____ assessment of group projects

    _____ grading on a curve

    _____ grading on a percentage basis

33. Examine the following list of student skills. Put a plus (+) in front of each item you consider to be one of your strengths. Put a minus (−) in front of each item you consider to be one of your weaknesses. If the item does not apply to you, leave it blank.

_____ reading skills   _____ oral communication skills

_____ scientific research skills   _____ library skills

_____ writing skills   _____ math skills

_____ comprehending instruction   _____ study skills

_____ completing assignments   _____ computer skills

_____ general problem solving skills

34. Examine the following list of support/services. Put a plus (+) in front of those that helped you during your enrollment at UND. Put a minus (−) in front of those that hindered you. If you are neutral or have no opinion, please leave the space blank.

_____ registration services   _____ library services

_____ placement services   _____ computer facilities

_____ orientation services   _____ counseling services

_____ tutoring services   _____ support from students

_____ child care services   _____ support from my family

_____ financial aid services   _____ support from instructors and advisors

_____ housing

_____ campus parking

35. Briefly describe the most difficult obstacle you've had to overcome in your current University studies. _____

_____

_____

_____

Thank you for taking the time to complete this form

Please return the completed form in the enclosed self-addressed stamped envelope to:

Mary Helen Pelton
Assistant Dean
Division of Continuing Education
c/o Bureau of Educational Services & Applied Research
University of North Dakota
Box 8158 — University Station
Grand Forks, ND 58202-9990

U N I V E R S I T Y   O F   **UND**   N O R T H   D A K O T A

OUTREACH PROGRAMS
DIVISION OF CONTINUING EDUCATION
BOX 8277, UNIVERSITY STATION
GRAND FORKS, NORTH DAKOTA 58202
1-800-342-8230 (ND ONLY)
FAX: 701-777-4282

ADMINISTRATION (701) 777-2661
ACADEMIC PROGRAMS (701) 777-4235
PROFESSIONAL AND COMMUNITY PROGRAMS (701) 777-2663
UND GRADUATE CENTER AT BISMARCK (701) 224-5437

March 15, 1988

Thomas J. Clifford
Twamley Hall - 300
University of North Dakota
Grand Forks, ND 58202

Dear Thomas:

I am writing you on behalf of the Adult Learning Consulting Group, an ad hoc University committee. The Consulting group is examining the differences in educational experiences and aspirations of University students of varying ages. As part of the study, we are surveying approximately six hundred students at UND and your name has been randomly selected to be a project participant.

We will send a questionnaire in approximately one week, and it will ask you for background information and information about your experiences as a student. Your answers to these questions will help the University better understand the problems and expectations of its students. You will need no more than fifteen minutes to complete the questionnaire.

In keeping with University policy on surveys such as this one, the answers you provide to the questionnaire will be analyzed in an anonymous manner. If you have any questions concerning this project, please feel free to call Mary Helen Pelton at 777-4225. Thank you for your help.

Sincerely,

Mary Helen Pelton, Ed.D.
Assistant Dean of Continuing Education

UNIVERSITY   OF   UNⅅ   NORTH   DAKOTA

OUTREACH PROGRAMS
DIVISION OF CONTINUING EDUCATION
BOX 8277, UNIVERSITY STATION
GRAND FORKS, NORTH DAKOTA 58202
1-800-342-8230 (ND ONLY)
FAX: 701-777-4282

ADMINISTRATION (701) 777-2661
ACADEMIC PROGRAMS (701) 777-4235
PROFESSIONAL AND COMMUNITY PROGRAMS (701) 777-2663
UND GRADUATE CENTER AT BISMARCK (701) 224-5437

March 22, 1988

Thomas J. Clifford
Twamley Hall - 300
University of North Dakota
Grand Forks, ND 58202

Dear Thomas:

Last week I wrote you describing the study being conducted by the
Adult Learning Consulting Group. Please recall that the Consulting
Group is examining the experiences and aspirations of University
students of varying ages. The survey's questionnaire is enclosed.

Would you please complete it at your earliest convenience and
return it in the enclosed stamped self-addressed envelope. Your
response will both contribute greatly to the Consulting Group's
work and be kept in strict confidence.

If you have any questions concerning this project, please feel free
to call Mary Helen Pelton at 777-4225.

Thank you!

Sincerely,

Mary Helen Pelton

Mary Helen Pelton, Ed.D.
Assistant Dean of Continuing Education

Enclosures

117

Adult Learners on Campus

U N I V E R S I T Y   O F   **UND**   N O R T H   D A K O T A

OUTREACH PROGRAMS
DIVISION OF CONTINUING EDUCATION
BOX 8277, UNIVERSITY STATION
GRAND FORKS, NORTH DAKOTA 58202
1-800-342-8230 (ND ONLY)
FAX: 701-777-4282

ADMINISTRATION (701) 777-2661
ACADEMIC PROGRAMS (701) 777-4235
PROFESSIONAL AND COMMUNITY PROGRAMS (701) 777-2663
UND GRADUATE CENTER AT BISMARCK (701) 224-5437

March 29, 1988

Thomas J. Clifford
Twamley Hall - 300
University of North Dakota
Grand Forks, ND 58202

Dear Thomas:

Two weeks ago I sent you a questionnaire prepared by the Adult Learning Consulting Group. Please recall that the Consulting Group is examining the experiences and aspirations of University students of varying ages. As of today, I have not received your completed questionnaire.

Would you please complete the questionnaire and return it in the stamped self-addressed envelope that accompanied it. Your response will both contribute greatly to the Consulting Group's work and be kept in strict confidence.

If you have any questions concerning this project, please feel free to call Mary Helen Pelton at 777-4225.

Thank you!

Sincerely,

Mary Helen Pelton

Mary Helen Pelton, Ed.D.
Assistant Dean of Continuing Education

Enclosures

U N I V E R S I T Y   O F   **UND**   N O R T H   D A K O T A

OUTREACH PROGRAMS
DIVISION OF CONTINUING EDUCATION
BOX 8277, UNIVERSITY STATION
GRAND FORKS, NORTH DAKOTA 58202
1-800-342-8230 (ND ONLY)
FAX: 701-777-4282

ADMINISTRATION (701) 777-2661
ACADEMIC PROGRAMS (701) 777-4235
PROFESSIONAL AND COMMUNITY PROGRAMS (701) 777-2663
UND GRADUATE CENTER AT BISMARCK (701) 224-5437

April 5, 1988

Dear Participant:

Approximately three weeks ago I sent you a questionnaire from the Adult Learning Consulting Group, and we have not yet received a completed form from you.

In case you did not receive the first questionnaire or have misplaced it, I have included another one with this letter. Would you please fill it out and return it in the self-addressed envelope at your earliest convenience.

Thank you on behalf of the Adult Learning Consulting Group. The information you provide will contribute greatly to the work of this Group.

Sincerely,

Mary Helen Pelton

Mary Helen Pelton, Ed.D.
Assistant Dean of Continuing Education

Enclosures

119

Annotated Bibliography:
Books on Adult Learners

In writing these annotations we have sought to (i) identify the purpose of the book; (ii) draw attention to its special features; and (iii) suggest who might best appreciate what it has to say. We do not feel this bibliography is an inclusive list of books on adult education; rather we see it as a sharing of books we have found useful.

We have used two terms in the annotations that need definition. *Practitioner* refers to people responsible for some aspect of adult education; practitioners include teachers, administrators, persons providing student services, etc. When we use the term *Scholars*, we are thinking of those who do research and write about issues associated with adult education. These terms are not mutually exclusive, and so we use them knowing that there are people who can well be described as both practitioners and scholars.

APPS, J.W. (1985) *Improving Practices in Continuing Education*, San Francisco: Jossey-Bass, 228 pp.
Apps provides a systematic and comprehensive approach to understanding the field of continuing education, and he explores ways of improving programs and practices and, in these regards, this book should be of interest to both practitioners and scholars. Apps also provides a concrete program evaluation allowing practitioners to examine their continuing education programs.

Although this book was written for the continuing education component of adult learning, Chapter 5 (Discovering new ways to view the adult learners), and Chapter 7 (Reconsidering current teaching and learning approaches) should be of special interest to anyone interested in the adult learner.

ASTIN, A.W. (1985) *Achieving Educational Excellence*, San Francisco: Jossey-Bass, 254 pp.
Astin examines the traditional criteria for excellence in higher education in the United States. He questions the practice of ranking institutions in a prestige hierarchy. He claims that the traditional assumptions about excellence are often counter productive, and that these criteria often interfere with the advancement of higher education. Astin proposes an alternate view of improvement, and he makes some suggestions as to specific changes which should result in improvement of student academic performance and faculty instructional skills. This book should be of interest to scholars in general and to administrators in particular.

ATCHLEY, R.C. (1987) *Aging Continuity and Change*, (2nd ed.), Belmont, CA: Wadsworth Publishing Company, 324 pp.
This book was written primarily as a gerontology text-book but should be of interest to anyone concerned with the adult learner. It helps the reader to understand the 'inner' experience of aging, and it provides a conceptual framework and information allowing the reader a better understanding of aging.

Atchley's book should be of particular interest to those concerned with adult developmental psychology and, as such, it will probably be of most interest to the scholar. This book provides an excellent glossary of terms as well as a good list of references.

BRIGHT, B. (Ed.) (1989) *Theory and Practice in Adult Education: The Epistemological Debate*, New York: Routledge, 288 pp.
There is a debate among those who would keep the conventional disciplines as they are now, through those who would maintain them but establish an informal praxis-oriented context, to the radical approach of abandoning the old disciplines altogether. This comprehensive book reviews the debate from each perspective in order to assess the theoretical basis for adult education curricula and professional practice. This book is useful to the scholar.

BROCKETT, R.G. (1988) *Ethical Issues in Adult Education*, New York: Teachers College Press, 218 pp.
This book addresses an often neglected area in the literature on adult learning — ethical issues. It explores topics from the vantage points of planning, administration, teaching, counseling, marketing, evaluation, and research. Rather than offering prescriptive solutions to specific ethical problems, the book aims to stimulate the reader's own ethical awareness and decision-making abilities.

BROCKETT, R.G., EASTON, S.E. and PICTON, J.O. (1988) *Adult and Continuing Education*, Phi Delta Kappa's Hot Topic Series, Bloomington, IN: Phi Delta Kappa, 310 pp.
This is a collection of 30 reprinted articles by leaders in the fields of continuing and adult education. The book is organized into four sections: (1) Overview, (2) Working with the adult learner, (3) Planning and administering adult and continuing education programs, and (4) Trends and issues. The section on trends and issues is particularly helpful as it brings together a collection of writings in an area of adult education that often receives only superficial attention. Also, Webster Cotton (in the overview) presents an informative twentieth century history of adult education. This book of readings is of greater appeal to the scholar than the practitioner.

BROOKFIELD, S.D. (1986) *Understanding and Facilitating the Adult Learner*, San Francisco: Jossey-Bass Inc, 376 pp.
This book is an examination and analysis of current approaches to adult learning. It presents a comprehensive review of how adults learn and proposes ways to develop adult education programs. The review of literature in each chapter is particularly good and constitutes a comprehensive list of references. The book should be useful to the scholar and the practitioner alike.

BROOKFIELD, S.D. (Ed.) (1988) *Training Educators of Adults*, New York: Routledge, 344 pp.
The purpose of this book is to help develop critically reflective practitioners of adult education — that is, educators who are aware of the assumptions underlying their practices and are capable of identifying theory underlying their practices. The twenty-five chapters, authored by a variety of authors (of both historical and current importance) are organized in eight sections. These eight sections move the reader from concepts and history through practice. The section on history includes reprints of the works of early adult educators and so provides valuable background for readers in the field of adult education.

CHICKERING, A.W. *et al.*, (1981) *The Modern American College*, San Francisco: Jossey-Bass, 810 pp.
Although this book is not written specifically for the adult learner, it is nevertheless a valuable resource for anyone interested in this population.

Even though this book is only a little over a decade old it has become a classic in the field. This book is comprised of forty-two chapters, written by a variety of authors, and organized into three sections (student needs; implications for curriculum; and consequences for teaching, student services and administration). The name index is a good review of the authorities in the field up to 1981. It will also be particularly helpful to those readers who are interested in adult development. Though this book may be of more interest to the scholar than the practitioner, it is useful to people with both kinds of interests.

CROSS, P.K. and MCCARTEN, A. (1984) *Adult Learning: State Policies and Institutional Practices*, ASHE-ERIC Higher Education Research Report No. 1. Washington, DC: Association for the Study of Higher Education, 152 pp.
This publication is an outgrowth of the Lifelong Learning Project funded by the W.W. Kellogg Foundation and so reports on considerations and experiments with appropriate roles for planning and delivering educational services for adults. It examined the range of problems confronting state agencies in planning for lifelong learning and investigated the roles available to them. This publication will be of interest to scholars and practitioners interested in governmental agencies.

DRESSEL, P.L. and MARCUS, D. (1982) *On Teaching and Learning in College*, San Francisco: Jossey-Bass, 214 pp.
Dressel and Marcus were concerned that college graduates often are not able to understand either the world around them or their social responsibilities. In light of these concerns, the authors addressed the following questions: How can students acquire knowledge? What kind of education will foster both human and skill development? What kind of college teachers and teaching are needed to meet this agenda?

The book is organized into three parts: (1) The purpose of education, (2) Teaching within disciplines, and (3) Bridging the disciplines. Though the book is not directed exclusively at adult learners, it nevertheless considers many issues that are applicable to the both older-than-average and traditional age students. This book is of interest to both the scholar and the practitioner.

FLAVELL, J.H. (1963) *The Developmental Psychology of Jean Piaget*, Princeton, NJ: D. Van Nostrand Co., Inc.
This classic book discusses Piaget's earlier and later work on the development of cognition, and ends with an evaluation of Piaget's systems.

FREEDMAN, L. (1987) *Quality in Continuing Education*, San Francisco: Jossey-Bass, 196 pp.
Freedman attempts to ensure quality in continuing education by establishing criteria by which to measure performance. To do this, he uses information he gathered through a comprehensive survey. He provides both theoretical and practical guidelines for improving program design, recruiting faculty and staff, establishing internal quality control, marketing and administration, and developing better relations between the 'traditional' higher education administration and continuing education. Although this book is primarily concerned with continuing education (one component of adult learning), it provides pertinent information for those interested in the broader view of lifelong learning. Chapter 2 (Adult learners and the campus student: Capabilities and performance compared), and Chapter 4 (Effective instruction: Competing views on how to teach adults) should be most beneficial for the practitioner.

GALBRAITH, W. (1990) *Adult Learning Methods*, Malabar, FL: Robert E. Krieger Publishing Co., Inc, 414 pp.
Malcolm Knowles, in the foreword to this book, states that 'This book is not only a how-to-do-it manual, but a what-to-do-and-why guide book'. It combines the writings of a variety of writers in the field (Conti, Wlofkowski, Long, Brookfield, etc.) in the process of undertaking a threefold task: (1) Understanding and facilitating the adult learner, (2) Methods and techniques, and (3) The future of adult learning. The methods and techniques section gives a good review of current and past approaches popular with adult educators — everything from learning contracts to nominal groups to internships. This book is of interest to both the scholar and the practitioner.

GROSS, R. (Ed.) (1982) *Invitation to Lifelong Learning*, Chicago: Follett Publishing Company, 288 pp.
Gross presents a collection of twenty-eight readings which examine lifelong learning. The diversity of the authors, past and present, adds to the richness of this book: Benjamin Franklin, Mortimer Adler, Margaret Mead, Carl Rogers, and Buckminister Fuller among others. Section III (Understanding Adult Learning) and Part IV (The Practice of Adult Education) will be of particular interest to those interested in teaching adults though the book will probably be of more interest to the scholar than to the practitioner.

HOULE, C.O. (1984) *Patterns of Learning*, San Francisco: Jossey-Bass Inc, 244 pp.
Houle examines the approaches to learning as a lifelong process. He examines the lives of great people as a way of investigating exemplary teaching and learning practices. He also discusses how adult learners can use traditional learning methods to improve contemporary programs, and he ties the book together with a chapter on implications for educators. This book has something for everyone but is perhaps of greatest interest to the scholar rather than the practitioner.

JARVIS, P. (1987) *Adult Learning in the Social Context*, New York: Routledge, 272 pp.
This book both offers a sociological model of adult learning and explores the meaning of adult education and, as such, will probably be of greatest interest to scholars. The book also received the 1988 Houle World Award for Literature in Adult Education. Jarvis' book arose from efforts of adults in analyzing their own education.

KNOWLES, M.S. (1977) *The Adult Education Movement in the United States* (2nd ed.), Huntington, NY: Robert E. Krieger publishing Company, 430 pp.
This book both chronicles the adult education movement and examines the role of adult education in the broader society. It is of particular interest as it is a revision of an early book on adult learners (first edition, 1962) and, as such, it helps the reader to recognize the changes within this movement. It is also interesting to note that andragogy, a concept addressed at great length in Knowles latter works, is only mentioned once in this volume. This book will be of greater interest to the scholar than to the practitioner.

KNOWLES, M.S. (1980) *The Modern Practice of Adult Education: From Pedagogy to Andragogy* (2nd ed.), Chicago: Follett Publishing Company, 400 pp.
In this book, Knowles moves from the theoretical to the practical. The theoretical is a comprehensive look at andragogy as opposed to pedagogy, and the practical are those educational implications evolving from andragogy. He makes specific suggestions which appear in his descriptions of contract learning, and program design and evaluation. This book is written both for scholars and for practitioners — scholars so they

understand Knowles at that point in time, and the practitioners because of the specific suggestions he makes.

KNOWLES, M.S. (1984) *Andragogy in Action*, San Francisco: Jossey-Bass, 444 pp.
Knowles explains how andragogy makes use of knowledge about what motivates adult learners and how they learn. This book examines how andragogy is applicable in a variety of settings: industry, government, higher education, continuing education, religious, education, and public schools. The introduction and the conclusion are written by Knowles while the remaining text is written by scholars and practitioners who apply andragogy to their particular area of education. Chapter one provides an excellent definition of andragogy as well as describing its applicability. This book will interest both the scholar and the practitioner.

KNOWLES, M.S. (1989) *The Making of an Adult Educator*, San Francisco: Jossey-Bass, 212 pp.
Malcolm Knowles recounts his fifty years in adult education in this book. He describes both his experiences and those people who affected his views of his world — whether professionally or personally. Because of his efforts in adult education, this book is both Knowles' autobiography and a recounting of adult education from his perspective. This book will be of greater interest to the scholar than the practitioner although Chapter 5 (Fifteen Questions That I Am Frequently Asked and the Answers I Give) will be of interest to both. The book also provides, in chronological order, an annotated listing of 197 of Knowles' articles.

KNOX, A.B. (1977) *Adult Development and Learning: A Handbook on Individual Growth and Competence in the Adult Years*, San Francisco: Jossey-Bass, 676 pp.
This book is a classic in adult education because it provides the first comprehensive review of both adult development and adult learning aimed toward people who are responsible for adult learners. While most adult education books treat the subject of development superficially if at all, this book considers the topic in detail appropriate to the needs of people responsible for teaching adults. And the chapter on the adult personality helps fill an important void in the adult education literature.

Knox moves from this psychological base to showing how psychological attributes of adults bear on adult learning. Furthermore, the novice researcher will be interested in the section on conducting research on adult development and learning (appendix). Although this book was published over a decade ago, it continues to be most useful in promoting the understanding of the adult learner.

KNOX, A.B. (Ed.) (1980) *Developing, Administering, and Evaluating Adult Education*, San Francisco, Jossey-Bass, 299 pp.
This book is written primarily for administrators of adult education programs. Knox and other contributors share exemplary practices in adult education and explore them from the perspective of concepts and procedures emerging from research and the adult education examined previously. The book also focuses on the increasing importance of the administrator in determining the success of a program.

Each of the nine chapters deals with topics of interest to an administrator. Topics range from the abstract (program objectives) to the practical (e.g., use of resources and staffing). Where this book will be of primary interest to practitioners generally, and administrators specifically, it will also be of interest to the scholar.

KNOX, A.B. (1986) *Helping Adults Learn*. San Francisco: Jossey-Bass, 262 pp.
This book is a comprehensive step by step guide in teaching the adult learner. Topics covered include the selection of the texts and other materials, building a supportive environment, selection of appropriate activities, selection of instructional techniques, strengthening institutional support for the adult learner, and evaluating the learner's experiences. Knox writes in a compelling manner, using 'real life' adult learners and situations to make his points. The book provides helpful and practical 'how to' advice — complete with checklists. The scholar will appreciate the excellent use of the literature in adult education.

LENZ, E.L. (1982) *The Art of Teaching*, New York: CBS College Publishing, 132 pp.
This is a 'how to' book meant primarily for those working directly with adult learners. While it doesn't have a strong theoretical base, it does make some very practical suggestions, and it also provides several sample evaluation forms for use in assessing faculty and program effectiveness. This book addresses the practitioner though it is probably most useful to the beginning practitioner.

LOVETT, T. (Ed.) (1988) *Radical Approaches to Adult Education: A Reader*, New York: Routledge, 320 pp.
The essays in this volume consider the contemporary radical adult education movement both as it appears in the context of the radical political movement, and within the history of radical politics and education. This collection of essays offers a broad theoretical and historical perspective on adult education and examines contemporary issues and initiatives using international examples. It seeks to tie the past with present theory and practice, along with offering new strategies for developing radical adult education. This book would be attractive to the scholar in adult education.

MCKEACHIE, W.J. (1978) *Teaching Tips: A Guidebook for the Beginning College teacher* (6th ed.), Lexington, MA: D.C. Heath and Company, 38 pp.
This popular book is meant for the practitioner — in particular, new college teachers. It addresses a wide variety of practical concerns: meeting the class the first time, choosing texts, preparing lecture notes, maintaining order, a variety of instructional techniques, evaluation, etc. Chapters usually begin with 'tips' and are followed by a discussion of the issues. This is very much a practitioner's book.

MERRIAM, S.S., and CAFFARELLA, R.S. (1991). *Learning in adulthood: A comprehensive guide*. San Francisco: Jossey-Bass.
This may be the best overview of adult learners available. Its sections examine the context and environment of adult learning, the adult as a learner, the learning process, the theoretical basis for adult learning, and some issues of current importance in adult education. The chapters dealing with the theoretical base are particularly helpful to the novice in adult education as they provide an excellent review of the various theoretical positions in the literature as well as giving an historical perspective. This book should be of interest to both practitioners and scholars.

PAPALIA, D., OLDS, S.W. and FELDMAN, R.D. (1989) *Human Development*, New York: McGraw-Hill.
This developmental psychology textbook provides an excellent overview of human development. This book devotes a section to young adulthood with a particularly good discussion of intellectual and identity development. This textbook should be of particular interest to scholars interested in the developmental issues as well as providing a helpful overview.

PASCARELLA, E.T. and TERENZINI, T.T. (1991) *How College Affects Students: Findings and Insights from Twenty Years of Research*, San Francisco: Jossey-Bass, 894 pp.
This book takes over where the classic work of Feldman and Newcomb (*The Impact of College on Students*, 1969) left off. In the intervening twenty plus years, the amount of empirical research added to the field is greater than all that reported in the preceding forty years, and this book attempts to synthesize the research in identifying the changes and benefits resulting from college attendance. Although this book does not deal exclusively with the adult learner population, many of the findings reported are pertinent to this population. This book will be most helpful to the scholar.

PERRY, W.G., JR., (1970) *Forms of Intellectual and Ethical Development in the College Years: A Scheme*, New York: Holt, Rinehart and Winston.
Perry, on the basis of a longitudinal study, interviewed students at a prestigious college. Based upon these interviews he formulated a theory of intellectual development which postulated formal operational levels of intellect and concurrent ethical development. Although this text is a classic on the developmental concerns of the traditional age college student, it is also most helpful to the scholar of the adult student.

SIMERLY, R.G. (1987) *Strategic Planning and Leadership in Continuing Education*, San Francisco: Jossey-Bass, 248 pp.
A variety of authorities with expertise in the area of continuing education share their approaches and programs in this book. Further, the book is written to show practitioners how to use strategic planning to formulate a successful program. The book takes a business approach with language reflecting this perspective — getting into the market, the parent organization, successful marketing, monitoring their competition, etc. This book will be of interest to practitioners generally, administrators in particular.

SCHLOSSBERG, N.K., LYNCH, A.Q. and CHICKERING, A.W. (1989) *Improving Higher Education Environments for Adults*, San Francisco: Jossey-Bass, 282 pp.
The authors of this book urge readers to be 'reflective practitioners' and provide information designed to allow this to occur. The book uses vignettes of 'real life' situations to make its points. Much of the book is dedicated to a description of the adult learner and the educational implications following from that description, and its second theme is institutional concerns which are also addressed. Both scholars and practitioners will find this book useful.

STEWART, D.W. (1987) *Adult Learning in America: Eduard Lindeman and his Agenda for Lifelong Education*, Malabar, FL: Robert E. Krieger Publishing Co., Inc, 290 pp.
This book examines Eduard Lindeman's philosophy of adult education ('Education is life'), a philosophy which is important because Lindeman was a pioneer in the field of adult education. Stewart gives special attention to the origin of adult learning in the United States.

This book is also of interest because Lindeman was Malcolm Knowles' first mentor and, through Knowles, had a great effect on adult education. This well researched book provides an excellent selected bibliography of the earlier works in adult education. The book is most attractive to scholars in the field of adult learning.

STUBBLEFIELD, H.W. (1988) *Towards a History of Adult Education in America: A Search for a Unifying Principle*, New York: Routledge, 208 pp.
Stubblefield describes the efforts of early theorists as well as the traditions that they helped establish. He discusses the continuing value of considering what they have written and shows how they provide vitality in the most contemporary of education. This book should be especially helpful to the scholar as it offers not only a sense of where adult education has been, but also an appreciation of where it is today.

TITMUS, C.J. (1989) *Lifelong Education for Adults: An International Handbook*, New York: Pergamon Press 590 pp.
This book includes 124 articles written by authors from twenty-three countries to examine the research and writing pertaining to lifelong learning for adults worldwide. The book is based upon updated and revised material from *The International Encyclopedia* first published in 1985. The book covers a wide range of topics (conceptual frameworks, purposes of adult education, teaching and learning, international organizations, and many more) and would be a helpful reference book for scholars in the field.

USHER, R. and BRYANT, I. (1989) *Adult Education as Theory, Practice, and Research.* New York: Routledge, 224 pp.
Usher and Bryant claim that even in the face of research, theory, and discussion in adult education, practice has changed little. And so they wrote this book in order to bring research and theory together in what they believe is a most productive way; the authors explore the interrelationships among theory, research, and practice. In doing this, they

bring these three aspects of adult learning together and offer a cohesive view of adult education. Although practice is a part of the title, this book will have the greatest appeal to scholars and not practitioners.

WEIMER, M. (1990) *Improving College Teaching*, San Francisco: Jossey-Bass, 232 pp.
This volume examines ways college administrators can provide faculty with the support, resources, and incentives they need to improve the quality of instruction. Although the intended audience is primarily administrators, Weimer also makes specific suggestions to teaching faculty. It is important to note that, while this book is not directed primarily at the 'older than average' student, many of the suggestions made are applicable to those interested in that population. The book would be of interest primarily to the practitioner — the administrator, in particular.

WHITBOURNE, S.K. (1986) *The Me I Know: A Study of Adult Identity*, New York: Springer-Verlag, 264 pp.
Whitbourne's book is an account of a study she did and the conclusions she drew from it. In this book, she challenges existing notions of adult development and change. Specifically, she questions existing theories which posit adult personality changes at predictable intervals; instead, she proposes that adults continuously strive within their own lives to verify the belief that life is good. Her study of ninety-four adult lives shows strong constancies in adult identity and the process through which individuals arrive at and maintain their views of themselves and their experiences. This book will be of interest to the scholar, particularly those who are interested in adult developmental psychology.

WLODKOWSKI, R.J. (1985) *Enhancing Adult Motivation to Learn*, San Francisco: Jossey-Bass, 314 pp.
This book treats the topic of motivation of adults. Wlodkowski analyzes six major factors that influence motivation: attitudes, needs, stimulation, emotion, competence, and reinforcement. He also demonstrates how motivation can improve instruction and increase learning in a wide variety programs. Wlodkowski addresses the motivational needs of both collegiate and industrial populations and should be of interest to both scholars and practitioners. The book also provides a good list of references on the subject of motivation of adults.

References

ALCIATORE, R.T. and ALCIATORE, P.L. (1979) 'Consumer reaction to college teaching', *Improving College and University Teaching*, **27**(2), pp. 93–95.

ANDREWS, T.E. (1981) 'Improving adult learning programs', in *Associations for Teacher Education* (Ed.) *Adult Learners: A Research Study*, Washington: Association for Teacher Education, pp. 11–29.

APPS, J.W. (1981) *The Adult Learner on Campus: A Guide to Instructors and Administrators*, New York: Jossey-Bass.

ARLIN, P.K. (1976) 'Toward a meta-theoretical model of cognitive development', *International Journal of Aging and Human Development*, **7**, pp. 247–253.

ASLANIAN, C.B. and BRICKELL, H.M. (1980) *Americans in Transition: Life Changes as Reasons for Adult Learning*, New York: College Board.

BACKUS, J.M. (1984) 'Adult student needs and university instructional practices', *Journal of Teacher Education*, **35**, pp. 11–15.

BASSECHES, M. (1980) 'Dialectical schemata', *Human Development*, **23**, pp. 400–421.

BEDER, H.W. and DARKENWALD, G.G. (1982) 'Differences between teaching adults and preadults: Some propositions and findings', *Adult Education* (USA), **32**(3), pp. 142–155.

BROOKFIELD, S.D. (1986) *Understanding and Facilitating Adult Learning*, San Francisco: Jossey-Bass.

BRUNER, J.S. (1966) *Towards a Theory of Instruction*, Cambridge: Harvard University Press, Belknap Press.

BUREAU OF THE CENSUS (1986) *Statistical Abstract of the United States*, Washington: Government Printing Office.

CARP, A., PETERSON, R. and ROELFS, P. (1974) 'Adult learning interests and experiences', in CROSS, K.P., VALLEY, J.R. and Associates, *Planning Non-traditional Programs: An Analysis of Issues for Post Secondary Education*, San Francisco: Jossey-Bass.

CHAMBERS, J.M., CLEVELAND, W.S., KLEINER, B. and TUKEY, P.A. (1983) *Graphical Methods for Data Analysis*, Belmont: Wadsworth.

COCHRAN, W.G. (1977) *Sampling Techniques* (3rd ed.), New York: John Wiley & Sons.

COMMONS, M.L., RICHARDS, F.A. and KUHN, D. (1982) 'Systematic and metasystematic reasoning: A case for levels of reasoning beyond Piaget's stage of formal operations', *Child Development*, **53**, pp. 1059–1069.

CONTI, G.J. (1984) 'Does teaching style make a difference in adult education?' *Proceedings of the Adult Education Research Conference*, **25**, Raleigh: North Carolina State University.

CROPPER, D.A., MECK, D.S. and ASH, M.J. (1977) 'The relation between formal operations and a possible fifth stage of cognitive development', *Developmental Psychology*, **5**, pp. 517–519.

CROSS, K.P. (1981) *Adults as Learners: Increasing Participation and Facilitating Learning*, San Francisco: Jossey-Bass.

DAMON, W.B. (1983) *Social and Personality Development*, New York: W.W. Norton & Co.

DARKENWALD, G.G. and MERRIAM, S.B. (1982) *Adult Education: Foundations of Practice*, New York: Harper & Row.

DEWEY, J. (1903) *Ethical Principals Underlying Education*, Chicago: Rand McNally.

DOUVAN, E. (1981) 'Capacity for intimacy', in CHICKERING, A.W. (Ed.) *The Modern American College*, San Francisco: Jossey-Bass.

DRAVES, W.A. (1980) *The Free University: A Model for Life Long Learning*, New York: Cambridge Books.

DUBIN, S. and OKIN, M. (1982) 'Implications of learning theory for adult instruction', *Adult Education*, **24**(1), pp. 3–19.

DUSEK, J., CARTER, O.B. and LEVY, G. (1986) 'The relationship between identity development and self-esteem during the late adolescent years', *Journal of Adolescent Development*, **1**, pp. 251–265.

DU TOIT, S.H.C., STEYN, A.G.W. and STUMPF, R.H. (1986) *Graphical Exploratory Data Analysis*, New York: Springer Verlag.

EBLE, K.E. (1972) *Professors as Teachers*, San Francisco: Jossey-Bass.

ERIKSON, E.H. (1961) 'The roots of virtue', in HUXLEY SIR J. (Ed.) *The Humanistic Frame*, New York: Harper and Row, pp. 145–165.

ERIKSON, E.H. (1968) *Identity, Youth, and Crisis*, New York: Norton.

EVANS, R.I. (1967) *Dialog with Erik Erikson*, New York: Harper & Row.

EVEN, M.J. (1982) 'Adapting cognitive style learning in practice', *Lifelong Learning: The Adult Years*, **5**(5), pp. 14–16.

EVEN, M.J. (1987) 'Why adults learn in different ways', *Lifelong Learning*, **10**, pp. 22–27.

FEUER, D. and GEBER, B. (December 1988) 'Oh-oh . . . second thoughts about adult learning training', *Training*, pp. 31–39.

FISHER, J.C. (1981) 'The relationship between anomia, life satisfaction and education-related variables among older adults', in WOOD, G.S. JR, and WOOD, A. (Eds) *Midwest Research-to-practice Conference in Adult, Community and Continuing Education*, Arlington, VA.

FLAVELL, J.H. (1963) *The Developmental Psychology of Jean Piaget*, Princeton, NJ: D. Van Nostrand Co., Inc.

GIESE, W. (1988) 'Four of the five of us say we enjoy going to work', in VANDER ZANDEN, J.W., *Human Development*, New York: Alfred A. Knopf, P. 522.

HAERTREE, A. (1984) 'Malcolm Knowles' theory of andragogy: A critique', *International Journal of Lifelong Education*, **3**, pp. 203–210.

HAMACHEK, D.F. (1986) *Psychology in Teaching and Learning, and Growth*, Boston: Allyn and Bacon, Inc.

HAVIGHURST, R.S. (1972) *Developmental Tasks and Education*, New York: McKay.

HOULE, C.O. (1972) *The Design of Education*, San Francisco: Jossey-Bass.

HUGHES, R. (1983) 'The non-traditional student in higher education: A synthesis of the literature', *National Association of Student Personnel Administrators Journal*, **20**, pp. 51–64.

IHEJIETO-AHARANWA, C.O. (1986) 'The role of interpersonal communication in teaching and learning situations', in WOOD, G.S. JR. and WOOD, A. (Eds) *Midwest Research-to-Practice Conference in Adult, Community and Continuing Education*, Arlington, VA.

JUNG, C.G. (1925) *Contributions to Analytic Psychiatry*, New York: Harcourt, Brace and World.

KASWORM, C. (1990) 'Adult undergraduates in higher education: A review of past research perspectives', *Review of Educational Research*, **60**, pp. 345–372.

KNOWLES, M.S. (1977) *The Adult Education Movement in the United States* (2nd ed.), Huntington, NY: Robert E. Krieger Publishing Co.

KNOWLES, M.S. (1980) *The Modern Practice of Adult Education: From Pedagogy to Andragogy* (2nd ed.), Chicago: Follett Publishing Co.

KNOWLES, M.S. (1984) *Andragogy in Action*, San Francisco: Jossey-Bass.

KNOX, A.B. (1976) 'Helping adults learn', in SMITH, R.M. (Ed.) *Adult Learning: Issues and Innovations*, Dekalb, IL: Northern Illinois University Information Program in Career Education, pp. 77–111.

KNOX, A.B. (1977) *Adult Development and Learning: A Handbook on Individual Growth and Competence in the Adult Years*, San Francisco: Jossey-Bass.

KNOX, A.B. (1980) *Developing, Administering, and Evaluating Adult Education*, San Francisco: Jossey-Bass.

KNOX, A.B. (1986) *Helping Adults Learn*, San Francisco: Jossey-Bass.

KOHLBERG, L. and GILLIGAN, C. (1971) 'The adolescent as a philosopher. The discovery of the self in a post conventional world', *Daedalus*, **100**(pt. 2), pp. 1051–1086.

KRAMER, D.A. (1983) 'Post formal operation? A need for further conceptualization', *Human Development*, **29**(26) pp. 91–105.

KRAMER, D.A. and WOODRUFF, D.S. (1986) 'Relativistic and dialectical thought in three adult age groups', *Human Development*, **29**, pp. 280–290.

LABOUVIE-VIEF, G. (1980) 'Beyond formal operations: Uses and limits of pure logic in life-span development', *Human Development*, **23**, pp. 141–161.

LEADBEATER, B. (1986) 'The resolution of relativism in adult thinking', *Human Development*, **29**, pp. 291–300.

LEVINSON, D.J., DARROW, E.M., KLEIN, E.B., LEVINSON, M.H. and McKEE, B. *The Seasons of a Man's Life*, New York: Knopf.

MACKIE, K. (1981) *The Application of Learning Theory to Adult Teaching*, Nottingham, England: Department of Adult Education, University of Nottingham.

MANNING, P.R. (1967) 'The programmed lecture: Programmed techniques for oral presentation to large groups', in LYSAUGHT, J.P. and JASON, H. (Eds) *Self-instruction in Medical Education*, Rochester, NY: The Rochester Clearinghouse on Self-Instructional Materials for Health Care Facilities.

MASLOW, A.H. (1970) *Motivation and Personality* (2nd ed.), New York: Harper and Row.

McCLUSKY, H. (1976) 'What research says about learning potential and teaching older adults', in ROBERD, M.T. (Ed.) *Adult Learning: Issues and Trends*, Dekalb, IL.: NIU Information Program.

McKEACHIE, W. (1978) *Teaching Tips for New College Teachers*, (7th ed.), Lexington, MA: D.C. Heath.

McLEISH, J. (1976) 'The lecture method', in GAGE, N.L. (Ed.) *The Psychology of Teaching Methods*, Chicago: National Society for the Study of Education.

MEZIROW, J. (1989) 'Personal perspective change through adult learning', in TITMUS, C.J. (Ed.) *Lifelong Education for Adults: An International Handbook*, Oxford: Pergamon Press.

MOORE, A.B. (1982) 'Learning and teaching styles of adult education teachers', *Proceedings of the Adult Education Research Conference*, **23**, Lincoln: University of Nebraska.

MORRISON, D.F. (1976) *Multivariate Statistical Methods*, New York: McGraw-Hill.

PAPALIA, D.E., OLDS, S.W. and FELDMAN, R.D. (1989) *Human Development*, New York: McGraw-Hill.

PERRY, W.G., JR. (1970) *Forms of Intellectual and Ethical Development in the College Years: A Scheme*, New York: Holt, Rinehart & Winston.

PHOENIX, C.Y. (1987) 'Getting them involved. Styles of high- and low-rated teachers', *College Teaching*, **35**, pp. 13–15.

PIAGET, J. (1967) 'The mental development of the young child', in ELKIND,

D. (Ed.) *Six Psychological Studies*, New York: Random House, pp. 88–98.

RIEGEL, K.F. (1976) 'The dialectics of human development', *American Psychologist*, pp. 689–700.

ROGERS, C.R. (1962) 'Towards becoming a fully functioning person', in *Perceiving, Behaving, Becoming. Yearbook of the Association of Supervision and Curriculum Development*, Washington D.C.: National Education Association.

Ross, J.M. (1989) *Critical Teaching Behaviors as Perceived by Adult Undergraduates*, American Educational Research Association annual meeting, San Francisco.

ROSS-GORDON, J. (1991) 'Critical indcidents in the college classroom: What do adult undergradutes perceive as effective teaching?' **55**, pp. 14–33.

RUBENSON, K. (1977) *Participation in Recurrent Education*, Paris: Center for Educational Research and Innovation, Organization for Economic Cooperation and Development.

SCANLAN, C.S. and DARKENWALD, G.G. (1984) 'Identifying deterrents to participation in continuing education', *Adult Education Quarterly*, **34**, pp. 155–166.

SCHMIDT, S.D. (1984) 'Examining the learning styles of returning adult students: Emerging elements of best practice with implications for teaching styles', *Proceedings of the Adult Education Research Conference*, **25**, Raleigh: North Carolina State University.

SLOTNICK, H.B. (1982) 'A simple method for collecting, analyzing, and interpreting evaluative data', *Evaluation in the Health Professions*, **5**(3), pp. 245–258.

SLOTNICK, H.B. and DURKOVIC, R.G. (1975) 'Dimensions of medical students' perceptions of instruction', *Journal of Medical Education*, **50**(7), pp. 662–666.

SNODDY, J.S. and LEVINE, S.J. (1986) 'Program evaluation in adult education: A survey of participants in a university summer program', in WOOD, G.S. JR. and WOOD, A. (Eds) *Midwest Research-to-practice Conference in Adult, Community, and Continuing Education*, Arlington, VA.

SNYDER, T.D. and HOFFMAN, C.M. (1991) *Digest of Educational Statistics, 1990*, Washington: National Center for Educational Statistics.

TOUGH, A. (1981) 'Interests of adult learners', in CHICKERING, A. (Ed.) *The Modern American College*, San Francisco: Jossey-Bass.

TUCKMAN, B.W. (1965) 'Developmental sequence in small groups', *Psychological bulletin*, **63**, pp. 384–399.

TUCKMAN, B.W. and JENSEN, M.C. (1977) 'Stages of small group development revisited', *Group and Organization Studies*, **4**, pp. 419–427.

VAN NESS, R. (1986) 'Factors affecting self-esteem in adult undergraduate students', in WOOD, G.S. Jr. and WOOD, A. (Eds) *Midwest*

Research-to-practice Conference in Adult, Community and Continuing Education, Arlington, VA.

WATERMAN, A.S. (1982) 'Identity development from adolescence to adulthood: An extension of theory and a review of research', *Developmental Psychology*, **18**(3), pp. 341–359.

Index